Do We Survive Death?

Dr David Hodges is a member of Ashford Preparative Meeting and an Elder of East Kent Monthly Meeting of the Religious Society of Friends (Quakers). A biological scientist and a university lecturer for more than 30 years - now retired, he has taught and researched in the fields of animal physiology and cell biology, as well as being involved in researching, practising and writing about spiritual healing.

Born in 1934, he was educated at a local Grammar School in Devon and at Exeter and London Universities. Following National Service he joined the staff of Wye College, the School of Agriculture of London University where, as well as conventional teaching and research, he became deeply involved in the organic farming movement, both nationally and internationally. He has authored, co-authored and edited books, conference proceedings and many research and review papers, as well as writing numerous more popular articles. He founded, and for 14 years edited, a scientific journal, *Biological Agriculture and Horticulture*, dedicated to the development of sustainable food production systems.

By the same author:

The Histology of the Fowl (1974)

The Role of Microorganisms in a Sustainable Agriculture (joint editor, 1986)

Science, Spirituality and Healing (1994)

Nitrogen Leaching in Ecological Agriculture (joint editor, 1995)

George Fox and the Healing Ministry (1995)

The symbol on the front cover signifies Karma – The Wheel of Law (*Buddhist*) and is reproduced by kind permission of Dover Publications Inc., New York USA

Do We Survive Death?

A descriptive bibliography and discussion on the evidence supporting survival

Second edition

Compiled and Written by
David Hodges

"There are more things in heaven and earth, Horatio,
Than are dreamt of in your philosophy."

Wm. Shakespeare *Hamlet* Act I Scene V

Published by David Hodges
in association with
The Pelegrin Trust

First edition published in 2001 by
Webbs Cottage Press
Woolpits Road
Great Saling, Braintree
Essex CM7 5DZ
UK

Second edition published in 2004 by
David Hodges
14 Eythorne Close
Kennington, Ashford
Kent TN24 9LP
UK

ISBN 0-9546122-0-5

Designed and typeset by Michael Gaze
in 10 on 12 pt Palatino Linotype

Printed and bound in Great Britain by
Crown Print and Design, Wye, Ashford
Kent TN25 5EE UK

To Ursula

for her love, support and understanding,
during the preparation of this book
- and always

࿓

To Clare
with every regard

[signature]

← !

Words of Wisdom

Contents

Acknowledgements

I am particularly grateful to the trustees of the Pelegrin Trust, whose generous grant provided most of the support needed for the production of the second edition, and to Jim Shields who also gave significant financial assistance.

My thanks are also due to Michael Gaze who gave his time to prepare the text for printing and also to Sir Charles Jessel and Michael Gaze for their invaluable help in editing the book.

I wish to record my thanks to the members of the Quaker Fellowship for After-Life Studies for their support in this project and for their individual contributions to the text and particularly to Angela and Martin Howard for their continuing support and help during its production.

I would like to express my gratitude to David Lorimer, Development Director of the Scientific and Medical Network for his permission to use seven of his mini-reviews of books on near-death experiences and also to Elizabeth Fenwick for the use of three of her mini-reviews on books about reincarnation.

I would like to thank the librarian of the College of Psychic Studies for help in finding some of the older literature.

I am also grateful to the following publishers or authors for the use in the text of short quotations from their books:

Pilgrim Books, Norwich for the use of a quotation from the foreword of Raynor Johnson (1984) *Light of All Life* and also for a quotation from the foreword from Paul Beard (1966) *Survival of Death*

James Clarke & Co. Ltd., Cambridge for the use of short extracts from Robert Crookall (1961) *The Supreme Adventure*

Eric Dobby Publishing Ltd., Barming Kent UK for permission to quote from Colin Wilson (1985) *Afterlife. An Investigation of the Evidence for Life After Death*

Hodder & Stoughton, London for a quotation from Sir Oliver Lodge (1931) *Past Years. An Autobiography*

Cambridge University Press, London for the use of a quotation from Caroline Spurgeon (1913) *Mysticism in English Literature*

Gill & Macmillan Ltd., Newleaf Press Dublin Eire for the use of material from Kathleen Dowling Singh (1999) *The Grace in Dying*

The Rudolf Steiner Press, London for the use of material from Rudolf Steiner (1999) *Founding a Science of the Spirit*

The Swedenborg Foundation (Chrysalis Books) West Chester USA for the use of material from Fox, L. & Rose, D.L. (1996) *Conversations With Angels. What Swedenborg Heard in Heaven*

The Swedenborg Society, London for the use of material from Emanuel Swedenborg (1989) *Heaven and its Wonders and Hell. From Things Seen and Heard*

The Editor of *The Friends Quarterly* for permission to quote from William Le Geyt "Swedenborg's Radical Christianity" *The Friends' Quarterly,* vol 19, no 1 (January 1975) pp 39-43

The Society for Psychical Research for permission to quote the Abstract from *"The Scole Report"* Proceedings of the Society for Psychical Research, vol 58, part 220 (Nov 1999) page 157 The Society wishes that the following disclaimer be included in full:

> *"Readers must be reminded at the outset that, although the SPR publishes and seeks to fund reputable research into psychic matters, in common with most scientific bodies it holds no corporate views. In consequence, all the material it publishes remains the responsibility of authors concerned, and must not be regarded as being endorsed by the Society or even as necessarily representing the opinions or convictions of the Society's Council or membership. Thus, although the present investigation was conducted by three senior SPR figures, we were acting throughout in our individual capacities."*

Miss Jennifer Howard, editor of the Quarterly Review of the Churches' Fellowship for Psychical and Spiritual Studies, for permission to reprint a review of Jane Sherwood (1991) *The Country Beyond* by Jean Snow from an issue of the Quarterly Review.

C.W. Daniel Co. Ltd., Saffron Walden Essex UK for permission to quote brief extracts from three books published by Neville Spearman Publishers, one of their imprints: Jane Sherwood (1964) *Post-Mortem Journal* Helen Greaves (1974) *The Wheel of Eternity* and Helen Greaves (1975) *The Dissolving Veil*

Souvenir Press Ltd., London for the use of short extracts from Melvin Morse & Paul Perry (1991) *Closer to the Light. Learning from Children's Near-Death Experiences*

Hastings House/Daytrips Publishers, Fern Park Florida USA for the use of a quotation from Karlis Osis & Erlendur Haraldsson (1997) *At the Hour of Death* [3rd edition]

Professor Gary E. Schwartz for permission to reprint the section entitled *"The Art of Mediumship: Personal and Professional"* which occurs on pages 362-363 of his book *The Afterlife Experiments: Breakthrough scientific evidence of life after death* Pocket Books New York USA (2002)

Professor Charles Tart for permission to quote a short passage from his paper in the *Christian Parapsychologist,* vol 13, no 7, pp 204-207 (1999)

The Curtis Brown Group Ltd., London on behalf of the Estate of Brian Inglis for permission to quote from Brian Inglis (1977) *Natural and Supernatural. A History of the Paranormal from Earliest Times to 1914* Hodder & Stoughton, London page 311 © Brian Inglis 1977

Arrangement of the Bibliography

The main contents of this bibliography have been divided into nine sections plus the Discussion and Personal Conclusions.

The core of each section consists of a series of books or reports, the references to which are given in as much detail as possible to enable those interested to track down the publication. For example, where available, ISBN numbers are included and where older books have been reprinted details may be given of both originals and reprints. The layout of the book details is explained in Figure 1. For a variety of reasons, not all books quoted may have full details cited. Usually a short description of the contents is given for each book. This may include, in parenthesis, some of the descriptive material originally supplied by the publishers, or from subsequent reviews – where this gives a realistic description of the contents. In the case of some of the more important sources, a more detailed description is given and the continuity of each section is maintained by a general commentary added where appropriate. In order to help those who feel unable to wade through the fairly extensive list of books covered in the bibliography, a short reading list is included at the end of the book (p 128). This list includes a few books which can be considered as essential reading – or as a straightforward introduction to the subject.

The final section of the bibliography consists of a general discussion of the subject of the survival of death as described in the published materials which have been considered, followed by personal conclusions. These conclusions are personal to the author since, in the final analysis, every individual considering the question of survival has to make their own decision about which way to interpret the evidence and whether or not they accept the idea of survival.

The author(s)

Date of this or first edition, always in brackets

Book title and sub-title, always italics

Myers, F.W.H. (1903) *Human Personality and its Survival of Bodily Death* **Longmans Green London**. An abridged version in one volume, leaving out much of the detailed case histories, was published 1919 **The abridged version has been reprinted by Pilgrim Books Norwich UK (1992) ISBN 0-946259-39-9** This latest printing contains the unabridged Epilogue from the original edition

Publisher(s) possibly printer/publishers

ISBN number which is a unique reference to the book or publication

Comments pertinent to the publication, always shown in plain type. Special information is in square brackets, eg [paperback] or [Dutch]

The country of origin is shown unless it is London - when this is assumed "London UK"

Please note that in some instances, the first publisher may differ from that shown

"ISBN" stands for International Standard Book Number. This number, when quoted, is assumed to be correct. Some entries are listed with alternatives "SBN" and "ISSN"

Punctuation is minimised intentionally within book references

Figure 1 EXAMPLE A book reference listing explained

≈

The Body of B. Franklin,
Printer,
Like the cover of an old book,
Its contents torn out
And
Stripped of its lettering and gilding,
Lies here
Food for Worms,
But the Work shall not be Lost,
For it Will as He Believed
Appear Once More
In a New and more Elegant Edition
Revised and Corrected
By the Author.

Benjamin Franklin (1706-1790) *Epitaph, written by himself*

≈

Foreword to the First Edition

More than 30 years ago I was introduced to the literature on the survival of death and spent some time reading a selection of the material described in the contents. At the time I was greatly impressed by the case supporting survival but did not continue further with the subject. Many years passed and I had followed up other lines of interest, allowing the concept of survival to remain relatively dormant in my consciousness. However, in 1999 this situation was changed by the publication of two small books by Quaker authors. These were, *Quakers & the Spiritual/Psychic Dimension* by Rosalind Smith[1] and *Continuing Life* by Angela Howard[2]. I was particularly interested in the latter as Angela Howard asked me to write the foreword to it, and this rekindled my interest in survival. In part of one sentence I stated that there is "...a considerable body of well-documented evidence supporting the validity of a belief in continuing life beyond death".

As a result of the publication of these books, in April 2000 a small group of Friends met together at Claridge House and decided to set up an informal group, the Quaker After-Life Studies Group (QASG), to explore the subject of survival further. One of the outcomes of this meeting was the decision to produce a bibliography of the main sources of evidence supporting the survival of death; and I agreed to undertake the production of the bibliography. I therefore found myself in the position where I had to justify my earlier contention about this "...considerable body of well-documented evidence..." What is set out in the main body of this document is the result of many months' work researching the various sources of information with the help and support of other members of the QASG. It is essentially only an outline of the evidence, quoting many of the main sources and accompanying these with a descriptive commentary to make the whole more than just a list of appropriate books to read. The final discussion and conclusions seek to give some depth to and to sum up the main body of the text.

To have sought to describe fully the great body of evidence favouring survival which is available would not have been possible in the context of what the QASG is seeking to do; which is to provide a straightforward and easily accessible introduction to the subject for Friends and others who wish to look into a subject that still, inexplicably, remains a *taboo* for many individuals. (It would also have been an encyclopaedic project beyond the inclinations or capabilities of any of the Group). It is hoped that there will be enough information provided here to set many readers off on a further exploration of a subject which, superficially, is fascinating but which, on a deeper level, is of fundamental importance to our individual spiritual growth and development.

David Hodges, March 2001

Foreword to the Second Edition

There are three main reasons for the production of this second edition of the Bibliography:

> The original text was researched and written to a rather tight deadline. The agreed need to have the booklet available at the same time as the Quaker Afterlife Studies Group's first day-conference on survival meant that pressures of time placed considerable restrictions on the amount of material that could be collected and processed.

> Subsequent to the time of publication considerable amounts of new material appeared as a result of earlier searches, much of which provided important support for the concept of survival. This meant that the first edition, although never intended to be a fully comprehensive account of the subject, was clearly suffering from significant 'holes' in the overall picture – holes which needed filling to ensure that the case for survival was being fully explored.

> The name of the Quaker After-Life Studies Group, who originally initiated this project, has been changed to the Quaker Fellowship for After-Life Studies (QFAS) and this updated edition is an appropriate reflection of the way in which the group has developed.

The new edition has been enlarged and improved in the following ways:

✦ A number of important texts have been included, particularly in the first, introductory, section.

✦ New sections or subsections dealing with Out-of-the-Body Experiences, apparitions and shamans and shamanism have been added.

✦ The Discussion chapter has been modified and extended.

✦ A range of quotations appropriate to the subject of survival and rebirth, see 'Words of Wisdom' (p vi), selected from across the world of literature, is included throughout the text. No attempt has been made to place any of these quotations in any order of merit, significance or of importance.

However –

✦ In spite of the value of medical literature, none of this material has been considered here because the bibliography has been specifically written to be of interest to a wider possible readership[3].

✦ This stricture has also largely been applied to the very wide-ranging psychical research literature that is found in specialist research journals and thus not readily accessible.

During the first half of 2002 several reviews were published commenting on the bibliography. Overall, it has been received very positively although one or two suggestions have been made for improvements. For example, it has been suggested that, particularly with the older literature, reference should be made as to whether or not the books remain in print. This was not done from the beginning for two reasons:

it would have meant a significant increase in the amount of research and enquiry needed to obtain the information[4];

information on books in print is only up-to-date for a very short while, since most publishers' book lists have a regular turnover and thus any list of this sort is essentially ephemeral.

It will be clear to those who have read the first edition that this bibliography is strongly inclined towards the belief that human survival of death is the most logical conclusion to be drawn from all the material under consideration. Indeed, the text is often written from the point of view that survival is more than just an hypothesis. I make no apology for this.

As indicated in the Discussion, the weight of opposition to the concept of survival – often with no substantial scientific evidence to support it – is so great that there is a need for those who do support this approach to life to speak out clearly in order that the evidence that is presently available should be more widely disseminated.

David Hodges, November 2003

Introduction

Amongst all the joys and problems of human life there is only one certainty: *that we all eventually must face death.* The obvious question which arises from this certainty is: does life end in oblivion and dissolution, or – as so many believe – does some part of us survive the process of physical death?

How we attempt to answer this question is very much dependent upon our personal belief system or philosophy of life and there are essentially three main approaches to developing an answer:

> The first of these is what modern, mainstream science accepts as reality: that there is nothing other than the material world we see around ourselves, that mind and consciousness are the result of the electro-chemical processes in our brains, and that when you're dead you're dead. This is the scientific materialist or humanist view and is believed to be 'the truth' by a large proportion of – but by no means all – western scientists and intellectuals. In relation to this, it is interesting to note that in recent years there has been the increasing interest and involvement of many scientists in previously 'fringe' areas, such as the relationship between consciousness and the brain and the study of phenomena which seem to be beyond the materialistic laws of cause and effect.

> The second approach, which is diametrically opposed to the first, is what has been believed at least as far back as historical records go in a wide variety of versions by probably the great majority of humanity. It is what we can call the traditional approach and is best exemplified by the 'Perennial Philosophy' which is the common thread underlying all the great world religions. In this, the material universe which is very real to us, is only secondary to a greater spiritual reality. We, as individual, eternal souls, are part of that greater reality. Each soul is born into a human body to live a life in the material world and eventually it dies 'out' of the body to return to the spiritual sphere. Many of those who accept this approach also believe that we have many lives – the doctrine of reincarnation. Such a view is usually rejected by materialists as a primitive belief but it has been and remains the majority view across the world.

> The third approach lies somewhere in the wide gap between the other two and often consists of no real approach to this question at all. Many people are so involved in earning a living, or raising a family, or just

getting by, that there seems to be no time or energy to give to such considerations. Others are often so involved in enjoying the material pleasures of life that they give no thought to where they come from and where they may eventually go. It is only when people are brought up short by some shock or calamity, personal or otherwise, that they ask why such things occur and, having no spiritual philosophy, are usually left inwardly floundering and hurt.

To anyone seriously considering which of the first or second approaches to the meaning of life is correct, the obvious question which comes to mind is: what is the evidence – *really sound evidence* – which supports either the humanist/materialist view of the world or the opposing traditional, spiritual world-view?

Although science through its discoveries is often considered to have disproved the reality of religion and spirituality – and it certainly has undermined many of the more superficial beliefs of traditional religion – in fact it has not been able to do so. A particular *interpretation* of the available evidence may suggest that the materialist view is the more likely explanation, but other interpretations may be equally or more valid.

The purpose of this review is to provide a descriptive bibliography of the books, reports and other sources of experience and evidence, both experimental and anecdotal, where the hypothesis of human survival of death is supported and discussed in a balanced manner. It also includes material not specifically concerned with the concept of survival but which provides support for it[5].

This review of the evidence has primarily been written for Quakers – members of the Religious Society of Friends. As members of a religious society, it might be assumed that Friends are willing to consider and discuss subjects such as death, dying and what happens thereafter. After all, such subjects must be included in a comprehensive spiritual world-view.

However, as in many other similar groups, there is a wide spectrum of belief and of acceptance as to what is appropriate to include in any statement of belief, whether personal or collective. It is hoped that many Friends who may feel uncertain about the subject of survival of death will take the time to look through this review and then dip into the recommended sources of information it includes, thus giving themselves a more informed basis on which to draw their own conclusions. It is also hoped that this material will be of value to a wider readership than just Quakers.

Footnotes: Forewords and the Introduction

[1] Smith, Rosalind (1999) *Quakers & the Spiritual/Psychic Dimension* Friends Fellowship of Healing ISBN 9-873048-43-2

[2] Howard, Angela (1999) *Continuing Life. The evidence for the survival of death through mediumship* Webbs Cottage Press Braintree Essex UK ISBN 1-899391-04-5

[3] There is often a considerable medical literature on some of the subjects in this study, for example, on Near-Death Experiences, and such material may put the subjects into a wider scientific context and also provide support for its spiritual interpretation.

[4] Most of the books reviewed here were obtained by borrowing copies from libraries – either the local branch of the County Library or from more specialised sources such as the library of The College of Psychic Studies – and I expected that most people seeking to explore the subject of survival would follow a similar path.

[5] The material available is very extensive and of variable quality. There are, for example, many 'popular' books which contribute very little to an objective debate. Thus, it has been necessary to be selective in what is included in this, relatively short, review. The present selection, being the choice of only a small group, may by chance miss some good examples of evidence. It would be helpful if any such examples not found here are drawn to the attention of the author for future inclusion.

I have been in many shapes
before I attained a congenial form.

Taliesin, (*Welsh Bard*)

୬

[The doctrine of the Essenes is] that souls…
are united to their bodies as in prisons, …
but that when they are set free from the bonds of the flesh,
they then, as released from a long bondage,
rejoice and mount upward.

Josephus. *Wars of the Jews,* ii, 8, 11

୬

Or ever the silver cord be loosed,
or the golden bowl be broken,
or the pitcher be broken at the fountain,
or the wheel broken at the cistern.
Then shalt the dust return to the earth as it was:
and the spirit shall return unto God who gave it.

Ecclesiastes xii, 6

❧

'The truest end of life, is to know the life that never ends.
He that makes this his care, will find it his crown at last.
And he that lives to live ever, never fears dying:
nor can the means be terrible to him that heartily believes the end.

For though death be a dark passage, it leads to immortality,
and that's recompense enough for suffering of it....

And this is the comfort of the good, that the grave cannot hold them,
and that they live as soon as they die.
For death is no more than a turning of us over from time to eternity.
Death then, being the way and condition of life,
we cannot love to live, if we cannot bear to die.

They that love beyond the world cannot be separated by it.
Death cannot kill what never dies.
Nor can spirits ever be divided
that love and live in the same Divine Principle,
the root and record of their friendship.
If absence be not death, neither is theirs.'

William Penn, Quaker, *Some Fruits of Solitude* 1693

❧

1 Introductory and General References

There are a number of books available which give either a short introduction to the subject of survival or which provide a substantial but not too detailed review of this field. There are also others which consider the subject in greater depth and with a more scientific or philosophical approach. Examples of both of these categories are described in this section, with the more detailed works being placed towards the end. Initially it is suggested, particularly to anyone seriously interested in the subject, that note be taken of a book published in 1988 by a scientist with considerable experience and knowledge. It is:

Ellison, Arthur J. (1988) *The Reality of the Paranormal* **Guild Publishing London ISBN 0-245-54474-7**

Professor Ellison was a retired professor of electrical engineering who had spent a great deal of his life investigating psychical research. He was twice President of The Society for Psychical Research and was widely experienced in the subject. His book is essentially his psychical research autobiography but is written in a very clear and readable style. At all times he remains objective and open-minded. Although he reviews the whole subject of parapsychology he nevertheless has much to say that is relevant to survival. In particular he makes the reader aware that many of the mediumistic phenomena associated with survival can be more easily explained on the basis of telepathy, etc. between sitter and medium. However, having done this, and in spite of his inherent 'scientific scepticism', he is left with the conclusion that: "...in my view the evidence for survival is exceedingly good..." Professor Ellison's book provides an excellent basis from which to set out on an exploration of the subject of survival.

Arthur Ellison's final book, published posthumously, in many ways follows on from *The Reality of the Paranormal* and brings his views on the paranormal in general and survival in particular right up to date. It is well worth reading together with his original book as an account of the experiences of a very knowledgeable psychical researcher. It is:

Ellison, Arthur J. (2002) *Science and the Paranormal. Altered states of reality* **Floris Books Edinburgh ISBN 0-86315-368-2**

A very straightforward and easily readable introduction to the subject is provided by:

Brookesmith, Peter (1989) ed *Survival of Death. Theories about the Nature of the Afterlife* **Macdonald & Co. London ISBN 0-7481-0298-1**

This is a large-format, fully illustrated book divided into seven main sections, each written by one or more authors. Each section deals with a major topic within the general subject area, but the decision as to what conclusions are drawn from the different aspects of the evidence is largely left to the individual reader.

The following two books together provide a valuable introduction to the subject of survival. The first sets the scene descriptively whilst the second considers the validity of the evidence for and against in some depth.

Currie, Ian (1978) *You Cannot Die. The incredible findings of a century of research on death* **Hamlyn London ISBN 0-600-32983-6 New impression published 1993 by Element Books Shaftesbury ISBN 1-85230-615-7**

Currie sets out the evidence for survival in a series of chapters on apparitions, hauntings, out-of-the-body experiences, deathbed visions, resuscitation experiences, reincarnation and descriptions of the afterlife. Each chapter is essentially composed of numerous accounts and case histories – that is the personal experiences of those who have been actually involved. It is basically a descriptive and informative, not an analytical and critical, account of the evidence.

Rogo, D. Scott (1986) *Life After Death. The case for survival of bodily death* **Aquarian Press Wellingborough ISBN 0-85030-504-7**

Rogo provides a good introduction to the field of survival covering all the main areas of evidence. In particular, since he had been closely connected with the research in these areas, his summaries of the early work in the field of the apparent communication with the dead via tape recorders and telephones (chapters 5 and 6) are of value. The author is by no means convinced of the reality of survival but, in the last sentence of the book, he states: "The case for survival is impressive, but not yet proven." However, since the mid-1980s when he wrote this conclusion, a great deal of further evidence supporting survival has appeared.

A fascinating history of the early years of the Spiritualist Movement and of psychical research, up to the 1920s can be found in:

Conan Doyle, Sir Arthur (1926) *History of Spiritualism* (2 volumes) **Psychic Press London. New edition 1989 also published by the Psychic Press 20 Earlham Street London WC2H 9LW ISBN 0-85384-078-4**

The author begins by describing the life of the Swedish visionary Emanuel Swedenborg (1688-1772) and concludes with a chapter on "Spiritualism and the War" with the story of the "Angels of Mons". He writes of the well-known mediums of the late nineteenth and early twentieth centuries and on all aspects of psychic phenomena and research. A proclaimed Spiritualist and leader of the Movement in its early days, he is extremely knowledgable on the subject and writes in his usual highly readable style.

Another interesting book by Conan Doyle is:

Conan Doyle, Sir Arthur (1930) *The Edge of the Unknown* **John Murray London**

This consists of fifteen chapters giving Doyle's thoughts, reminiscences and conclusions on a wide range of topics related to survival and spiritualism. It has value in that his comments come from one who was often deeply involved at the time and who personally knew many of the individuals concerned. Probably the two most interesting chapters are: Chapter I analysing the work and personality of Houdini; and Chapter XI summarising the research on ectoplasmic materialisation.

Paul Beard has written a trilogy of books which carefully assess and analyse the evidence for and against the survival of the human soul after death. Having been a member of the Society for Psychical Research for many years and the President of the College of Psychic Studies for 16 years, he made a lifetime study of psychical research. He was someone with the knowledge and experience to review the subject in a balanced way, quoting widely from many well-known writers as well as from other less accessible sources such as the archives of the Society for Psychical Research. The books are:

Beard, Paul (1966) *Survival of Death* **Hodder & Stoughton London. Now available in a 1988 impression from Pilgrim Books Lower Tasborough Norwich NR15 1LT ISBN 0-946259-25-9**

A good assessment of this book was written in the Foreword by Leslie Weatherhead: "Mr. Beard offers evidence with a quality of analytical detachment, which, to my mind, is exactly what is so badly needed. In the end he regards the evidence as sufficiently conclusive to warrant belief in survival, but he examines every possible alternative interpretation of the phenomena and is never woolly, or afraid of where his investigations may lead. He concedes every possible claim that telepathy and clairvoyance may account for many alleged "messages from the dead", but he finds a residue in the evidence for which the most intelligent and reasonable explanation is that of survival".

Beard, Paul (1980) *Living On. A study of altering consciousness after death* **George Allen & Unwin London ISBN 0-04-133009-9 Now available from Pilgrim Books (1987) ISBN 0-946259-24-0**

The author presents some of the evidence for continuing life, analysing the material and making comparisons. He discusses the evidence we possess about the quality and meaning of life beyond death.

Beard, Paul (1986) *Hidden Man* **Pilgrim Books ISBN 0-946259-16-X**

Paul Beard studies the contribution of discarnate teachers who seek to clarify something of the meaning and worth of the human journey through many lifetimes.

Iverson, Jeffrey (1992) *In Search of the Dead. A scientific investigation of evidence for life after death* **BBC Books London ISBN 0-563-36123-9**

An interesting and informative description of some of the more important evidence supporting survival. Somewhat popularised, it was the book of a BBC television series.

It is based largely on a series of specific cases or individual stories of events which relate to the possibility of survival; it is not a detailed study of the evidence. Nevertheless the author does quote some very telling passages from interviews he had with leading figures in the field.

Dr Raynor Johnson was born at the beginning of the 20th century. He trained as a physicist and held teaching posts in Queen's University, Belfast and King's College, University of London. At the relatively young age of 34 he was appointed Master of Queen's College in the University of Melbourne. His scientific background was therefore impeccable. As well as being a scientist, however, he also studied psychology, psychical research and mysticism, believing that "…the scientific attitude points beyond rationalism to the direct apprehension of spiritual reality." During the 1950s, '60s and '70s he wrote several books in which, seeking for a reasonable philosophy of life, he sought to explore and integrate three fields of enquiry – natural science, psychical research and mystical experience. His books, now classics, are as important now as when they were written over 40 years ago and are well worth reading in their entirety. However, certain chapters in three books make excellent introductions to the subject of survival and what happens to the human soul after death. These are:

Johnson, Raynor C. (1953) *The Imprisoned Splendour. An approach to reality, based upon the significance of data drawn from the fields of Natural Science, Psychical Research and Mystical Experience* **Hodder & Stoughton London. New impression published by Pelegrin Trust ISBN 0-946259-30-5 Available from Pilgrim Books Lower Tasburgh Norwich NR15 1LT**

A general discussion on the nature of reality, including chapters on The Survival of Death (Ch 13), Pre-existence, Reincarnation and Karma (Ch 18) and the Purpose of Human Life (Ch 19).

Johnson, Raynor C. (1957) *Nurslings of Immortality* **Hodder & Stoughton London. New impression published by Pelegrin Trust ISBN 0-946259-43-7 Available from Pilgrim Books**

The sequel to *The Imprisoned Splendour,* this book is an interpretation of the universe in terms of the philosophy of imaginism, the concept that Divine Imagination creates and sustains the universe. As well as surveying psychical research, Johnson includes chapters on The Adventure of Being Man (Ch 9), The Nature of the "Next Life" (Ch 12) and Cosmic Life: Group Souls (Ch 13).

Johnson, Raynor C. (1963) *A Religious Outlook for Modern Man* **Hodder & Stoughton London. New impression published by Pelegrin Trust ISBN 0-946259-27-5 Available from Pilgrim Books**

His re-interpretation of religion, particularly Christianity, in the light of modern science and psychical research. The final chapters cover subjects very pertinent to the present theme, such as the survival of death, the after-death state, the concept of rebirth and the meaning of human life.

Johnson, Raynor C. (1984) *Light of all Life. Thoughts towards a philosophy of life* **Pilgrim Books Norwich ISBN 0-946259-07-0**

Dr Johnson's final book, a series of lectures given in 1976 and printed as a British edition in 1984, it is the culmination of all his thinking and seeking throughout a long life.

As Paul Beard says in the Foreword in this book, Johnson "...reaches the summit of his quest, where the crown of life is seen as the willing surrender to a meaning beyond any the intellect can work out for itself, but which, when experienced by the whole man, then finds a willing acquiescence in the intellect too." In particular, it contains chapters on The Certainty of Survival of Death and The Soul's Great Journey.

An excellent and balanced survey of psychic phenomena in general has been written by **Brian Inglis**. In two volumes he provides "a detached historical survey" of the paranormal from earliest times up to 1939. His comprehensive coverage provides a lot more detail and background information than is normally found in popular works.

Inglis, Brian (1977) *Natural and Supernatural. A history of the paranormal from earliest times to 1914* **Hodder & Stoughton London ISBN 0-340-20526-1**

Inglis, Brian (1984) *Science and Parascience. A history of the paranormal, 1914 - 1939* **Hodder & Stoughton London ISBN 0-340-26325-3**

A revised edition of the first volume was published later:

Inglis Brian (1992) *Natural and Supernatural. A history of the paranormal from earliest times to 1914* **Prism Press Bridport Dorset UK**

Strangely enough, for what seeks to be a comprehensive survey, Inglis does not mention the important Canadian research undertaken by Glen Hamilton in the 1920s.

Colin Wilson is a prolific author, having written more than 50 books across a wide variety of fields, including science, literature, philosophy, psychology and criminology. However, among his chief interests have been the subjects of mysticism, the occult and the paranormal. In the field of the paranormal he has written nine books and he has been exploring and researching this subject for more than 20 years. Two of his books are of particular value for this review. They are:

Wilson, Colin (1985) *Afterlife. An investigation of the evidence for life after death* **Harrap Ltd. London ISBN 0-586-06628-4 Also published by Granada, London (1988) same ISBN**

Wilson reviews the evidence for survival in a very balanced, objective and readable manner; his book is well worth reading. He does not personally declare himself convinced of the reality of survival, although he says that the evidence points unmistakably towards that conclusion. At the end of the last chapter he states: "It is not my purpose to try to convince anyone of the reality of life after death: only to draw attention to the impressive inner consistency of the evidence, and to point out that, in the light of that evidence, no one need feel ashamed of accepting the notion that human personality survives bodily death."

Wilson, Colin (1988) *Beyond the Occult. Twenty years' research into the paranormal* **Bantam Books London ISBN 0-593-01174-0**

This book is not specifically about survival. It is an attempt by Wilson to summarize all that he has learned over 20 years about the paranormal. It contains much material dealing directly with the subject of survival and a great deal of useful discussion about how all the pieces of the 'paranormal jigsaw puzzle' may fit together. He puts forward a powerful case "…that our so-called 'normal' experience may in fact be sub-normal, and that evolution may have brought us near to the edge of a quantum leap into a hugely expanded human consciousness."

Lorimer, David (1984) *Survival? Body, mind and death in the light of psychic experience* **Routledge & Kegan Paul London ISBN 0-7102-0003-X**

David Lorimer's wide-ranging study of the possibility of our survival of death deals firstly with a review of the beliefs concerning the nature of life and death, moving from primitive attitudes through to modern philosophers and neurologists. The second part of the book, a short chapter, examines the ways that people think about the paranormal and what can be considered as evidence. The third part is an account of the empirical evidence which supports survival – apparitions, out-of-the-body experiences, near-death experiences and descriptions of bodily death. It argues that only a hypothesis involving conscious survival of bodily death provides a complete and coherent explanation of such evidence.

A valuable synthesis of a whole range of psychic communications suggesting survival has been published in:

Crookall, Robert (1961) *The Supreme Adventure. Analyses of psychic communications* **James Clarke & Co. London. Published for the Churches' Fellowship for Psychical Study**

In a very scholarly work, Dr Crookall has reviewed the literature describing experiences relating to the periods before, during and after death. He considers that, "…by means of analyses of psychic communications … it is possible to pierce the veil that obscures death and the immediate hereafter. Such analyses not only indicate *survival*: they also provide a means by which we can envisage *the general conditions under which we survive* and enable us to adduce *reasons why certain experiences are undergone at certain stages in the process of disembodiment."*

After a very scientific analysis and discussion of all the material the author comes to the conclusion that: "The whole of the available evidence is explicable only on the hypothesis of the survival of the human soul in a Soul Body. There is no longer a 'deadlock' or a 'stalemate' on the question of survival. On the contrary, survival is as well established as the Theory of Evolution."

Hart, Hornell (1959) *The Enigma of Survival. The case for and against an after life* **Rider & Company London**

Hornell Hart was Professor of Sociology at Duke University, North Carolina for many years. He also developed an interest in psychology and parapsychology; his own studies and his assessment of the evidence led him to a belief in survival. This book is a balanced and clearly stated review of both the pro- and anti-survivalist cases based on the main strands of evidence available at the time of writing. Although favouring the pro-survival case, Hart goes out of his way to ascertain and clearly state the arguments against survival and then compares the two, pointing out the weaknesses of the anti-survival case. It is a classic analysis of the subject and one which should be read by all serious enquirers. David Lorimer concludes: "The final chapter is a masterly summary of the case for and against [survival], showing that the will to (dis)believe is usually critical". In other words it is often our preconceived views, rather than the evidence, which decides how we respond to the concept of survival.

Almeder, Robert (1992) *Death and Personal Survival. The evidence for life after death* **Littlefield Adams Maryland USA ISBN 0-8226-3016-8**

The author is a philosopher who has carefully examined and weighed up the evidence for survival. He has examined the best material from the fields of reincarnation studies, possession, apparitions of the dead, out-of-the-body experiences, near-death experiences and trance mediumship and, having assessed the results in relation to the range of criticisms put forward by sceptics, he concludes that we now have compelling empirical evidence for belief in the survival of death. A very well argued book which is an excellent contribution to the literature.

ॐ

Becker, Carl B. (1993) *Paranormal Experience and Survival of Death* **State University of New York Press Albany NY USA ISBN 0-7914-1476-0**

Professor Becker's book is an extensive survey of more than a century of research into the paranormal and its implications for survival. As David Lorimer has stated, it is: "A superb overview of the evidence and arguments..." It also examines the reasons for the taboos on scientific discussion of psychical/survival research and suggests a new model for a more holistic view of the field. The author, rather cautiously, concludes there is good evidence that some individuals have survived in the past and, by inductive reasoning, that some people now alive will continue in conscious experience after the death of the body. The whole is well referenced and provided with an extensive bibliography.

ॐ

Roy, Archie E. (1996) *The Archives of the Mind* **SNU Publications Stansted Essex ISBN 0-902036-13-0**

Professor Roy is a scientist, astronomer and psychical researcher of considerable distinction. In this his second book on the paranormal his intention is to deliberately challenge those who are sceptical about these phenomena. To do so he describes in detail a relatively small number of cases from many sources which have been investigated by highly qualified investigators – and which clearly demonstrate the reality of the paranormal and thus of survival. His choice of cases is such that they are entirely convincing and really speak for themselves.

   In his Foreword to the book Colin Wilson states that the cases Roy quotes provide "virtually watertight evidence" which allows the sceptics very little room for criticism; and describes the book as "one of the most powerful and convincing books on the paranormal" since Frederic Myers' 1905 *Human Personality and the Survival of Bodily Death.*

ॐ

A very useful and up-to-date survey of the evidence for survival can be found in a website produced by an Australian, **Victor Zammit**, in 1999. Dr Zammit is a retired Solicitor of the Supreme Court of New South Wales and the High Court of Australia who is formally qualified in three university disciplines, psychology, history and law. He also describes himself as a psychic researcher and lecturer in psychic phenomena. In 117 pages of text, entitled *"A Lawyer Presents the Case for the Afterlife. The Irrefutable Objective Evidence"*, Dr Zammit analyses the evidence for survival from the point of view of a lawyer in court. In other words would the evidence be accepted in a criminal court as being beyond reasonable doubt – a standard of evidence which, until recently, was enough to hang a man. But he goes beyond this, having "…carefully selected aspects of psychic research and afterlife knowledge which would technically constitute objective evidence … in every civilised legal jurisdiction around the world." He comes to the conclusion that " …the evidence *taken as a whole* constitutes overwhelming and irrefutable proof for the existence of the afterlife." A very interesting and informative, if sometimes idiosyncratic, account of the evidence and one which has been of value in the construction of this bibliography.

> Dr Zammit's website is http://www.ozemail.com.au/~vwzammit *"A Lawyer Presents the Case for the Afterlife"*

> Printed versions of the text can be obtained from: Association for Scientific Investigation of the Afterlife PO Box 168 Double Bay 2028 NSW Australia, for the sum of $(Aus)10 plus $(Aus)7 postage (overseas).

Michael Roll is another individual who, for many years, has been treading a lone path trying to promote the evidence for survival to the widest possible audience through his organisation the **Campaign for Philosophical Freedom**. He runs an informative and outspoken website – www.cfpf.org.uk – and can also be contacted directly at: 28 Westerleigh Road Downend Bristol BS16 6AH. Amongst other things he distributes the books written by **Ron Pearson**, who has produced a physical/mathematical theory which seeks to put the concept of survival on a sound scientific footing. (See p 117)

Other very useful websites considering the evidence for survival are:

> **The International Survivalist Society** www.survivalafterdeath.org The ISS is a recent development, being founded in April 2002, which describes its purpose as "disseminating the Scientific Case for Survival After Death on a Global Level". It produces an excellent website which provides a regularly changing variety of historical material on, and evidence for, survival. One of the best sites on the internet, particularly for those starting out in the field of survival.

Scientific Support for Evidence Based Mediumship, Life After Physical Death and After Death Communication http://www.survivalscience.org/ This site consists of a wide-ranging list of websites which have been carefully reviewed and selected as providing scientific support for the "existence of religious beliefs concerning resurrection, eternal life and the existence of spirit, as well as help support scientifically all genuine evidence-based mediumship and the concept of life after physical death and after death communication."

Our birth is but a sleep and a forgetting;
The Soul that rises with us, our life's Star,
Hath had elsewhere its setting,
And cometh from afar.
Not in entire forgetfulness
And not in utter nakedness,
But trailing clouds of glory do we come
From God who is our home.
Heaven lies about us in our infancy!

William Wordsworth. *Intimations of Immortality*

ॐ

Souls departing hence exist there, and return hither again.

Plato. *Phaedo* (70)

ॐ

I hold that when a person dies
His soul returns again to earth;
Arrayed in some new flesh-disguise,
Another mother gives him birth.
With sturdier limbs and brighter brain
The old soul takes to the road again.

John Masefield. *A creed.*

12

2 Direct Research
The Major Sources of Research Directly Supporting Survival

The modern interest in psychic phenomena, particularly those associated with survival and usually demonstrated by mediums in a trance state, began over 150 years ago. The Fox sisters in America are usually considered to have initiated this trend when, in 1848, they apparently contacted the spirit of a man who had lived in their house and had been murdered there. A wave of interest in such activity spread rapidly across the western world, with genuine mediums producing apparently substantial psychic phenomena inextricably mixed with fraudulent mediums. The latter were out to make money from the bereaved seeking contact with their dead relatives. An important spin-off from this activity was the development of research into psychic phenomena, often undertaken by thoroughly sceptical scientists, and others, with the intention of showing that all mediums and their activities were fraudulent. Thus in 1882 the Society for Psychical Research (SPR) was founded in Britain, shortly followed by the American Society for Psychical Research. As well as these organised research groups there were many individual researchers who often undertook lengthy investigations into individual mediums. Examples of such individuals are the well-known scientists Sir William Crookes, Sir Oliver Lodge and Professor Charles Richet. Although these researchers often remained sceptical about psychic phenomena, having found nothing which convinced them of the reality of survival, there were many, often very high-profile scientists, who became convinced by their results that mediums were able to manifest phenomena which were inexplicable in mainstream scientific terms. Some of these accepted that the only realistic explanation was that the human spirit survived death. The more important books describing research of this sort are summarised below.

Sir William Crookes. One of the outstanding scientists in Europe during the second half of the nineteenth century was Sir William Crookes (1832-1919). A largely self-taught man, his scientific achievements and honours were legion. He was also initially a sceptic on psychic phenomena who undertook to examine some of the mediums who were active during the 1860s and 1870s and this work was the first systematic attempt to use scientific techniques in psychic research. Daniel Dunglass Home was the most famous physical medium of the time who was able to manifest a remarkable range of physical phenomena, which nobody had ever been able to demonstrate as fraudulent. Home had agreed to be tested under laboratory conditions using apparatus specially designed by Crookes. Under these conditions Home was able to demonstrate, for example, psychokinetic effects at a distance which were clearly measurable instrumentally.

Another medium Crookes investigated was Florence Cook who, in many séances, manifested the materialised form of 'Katie King' who was able to communicate at length with the other sitters. These investigations overcame Crookes' doubts and convinced him of the reality of psychic phenomena and the claims of the spiritualists. He published an account of his work in:

Crookes, Sir William (1874) *Researches in the Phenomena of Spiritualism* **J. Burns London**

An updated and augmented edition of this book was published as:

Crookes, William (1926) *Researches in the Phenomena of Spiritualism. Together with a portion of his presidential address given before the British Association 1898 and an appendix by Sir Arthur Conan Doyle* **The Two Worlds Publishing Co. Manchester UK and the Psychic Bookshop London**

A more recent review of his work is:

Medhurst, R.G. and Goldney, K.M. (1972) *Crookes and the Spirit World. A collection of writings by or concerning the work of Sir William Crookes, OM FRS in the field of psychical research* **Souvenir Press London ISBN 0-285-62037-1**

Although Crookes' work with D.D.Home was largely accepted at the time – even by some sceptical scientists – his results with Florence Cook, probably because of their almost unbelievable content, were considered unacceptable by many and were accordingly denigrated by his critics.

Sir Oliver Lodge. Like Sir William Crookes, Oliver Lodge (1851-1940) was one of the leading scientists of his generation. He was a physicist, among many other things being the first person to transmit a radio signal (one year before Marconi did so), and received international recognition for his work. He was awarded many honours and honorary degrees and was knighted for his services to physics and higher education. He was a Fellow of the Royal Society and was twice elected President of the Society for Psychical Research.

Again, like Crookes, Lodge was initially sceptical but recognised that there was much worth investigating in the mass of psychic phenomena which was appearing in the latter years of the nineteenth century. Thus, in parallel with his conventional work in physics, he undertook research into mediums and mediumistic phenomena, particularly with Mrs. Leonora Piper and Eusapia

Palladino [sometimes spelt Paladino]. Eventually he became convinced of the validity of much of this psychic material and of the reality of the survival of death. He wrote several books from 1909 onwards into the 1930s dealing at least partially with these subjects. Some of these are as follows:

Lodge, Sir Oliver (1909) *The Survival of Man. A study in unrecognised human faculty* **Methuen & Co. London**

Lodge gives an account of many of his investigations into matters connected with psychical research during the previous quarter of a century. He covers work on telepathy, automatic writing, trance speech and other instances of 'temporary lucidity', in which areas he considered that the most direct evidence for survival and after-death activity would be likely to be found. He reserved an account of his experiences with the more controversial and "often discredited" physical phenomena for another book. He makes it clear that, by this time, he was convinced of man's survival of bodily death.

Lodge, Sir Oliver (1916) *Raymond or Life and Death* **Methuen & Co. London**

The account of his son's death in the first World War in 1915. Lodge was already known for his work in psychical research and belief in survival. Part One of the book documents the life of Raymond and the events leading up to his death. Part Two documents the successful attempts of the family to make contact with the discarnate Raymond through mediumship. Part Three concerns Lodge's beliefs about the after-life and its philosophy.

A much revised and improved edition of the original with additional material and explanations of some originally contentious points was published in 1922. Overall much of the earlier edition was shortened and simplified without any loss of evidential value:

Lodge, Sir Oliver (1922) *Raymond Revised. A new and abbreviated edition of "Raymond or Life After Death" with an additional chapter* **Methuen & Co. London**

Lodge, Sir Oliver (1931) *Past Years. An Autobiography* **Hodder & Stoughton London**

A general account of his life, family and background which only contains a relatively short account of his work in psychical research. One chapter is given over to "The Ether Experiments" which he states to be "...the most important series of experiments in my life,". In the last chapter, his *"Apologia pro vita mea"*, he states: "My testimony, and that of others, to *the reality of a spiritual world is based upon direct experience of fact, and not upon theory.* [Emphasis added Ed.] "Test the facts whatever way you choose, they can only be

15

accounted for by the interaction of intelligences other than our own. Intelligences there appear to be of every grade, some of them possessing powers unknown to us."

Lodge, Sir Oliver (1933) *My Philosophy. Representing my views on the many functions of the Ether of Space* **Ernest Benn London**

This is a fascinating book. In it Lodge seeks to condense a lifetime's work at the forefront of both physical science and psychical research and to produce a personal philosophy which integrates the materialistic outlook of modern science with spirituality and the traditional religious outlook of humanity. The key factor in his philosophical approach is the Ether; as he states: "The Ether of Space has been my life study, and I have constantly urged its claims to attention." He believed that the Ether provides the link between the material universe and the spiritual world which is demonstrated, however unclearly, by psychical research. The importance of the Ether in his life's work is encapsulated in the statement that: "…when in my old age I came to write this book, I found that the Ether pervaded all my ideas, both of this world and the next. … and now I find it has grown into a comprehensive statement of my philosophy." Unfortunately, at the time of writing he had arrived at a: "…day when the universe by some physicists seems resolved into mathematics, and the idea of an Ether is by them considered superfluous, if not contemptible." Regrettably, this remains the position today 70 years after Lodge wrote these words (but see pp 116-118).

The Cross-Correspondences

Some of the best work that has been undertaken which strongly supports the idea of survival is that which has been termed the "Cross-Correspondences". What is so remarkable about this research is that, if the survival hypothesis is accepted, the work was planned and undertaken 'post-mortem'; i.e. the individuals who designed and performed the experiments were already dead when they undertook the work. F.W.H. Myers was a classical scholar and a founder member of the Society for Psychical Research who died in 1901. About five years later, and continuing for the following 30 years, more than 2000 automatic scripts were produced which when transmitted to different mediums across the world as separate fragments seemed incomprehensible, but which, when brought together and integrated and analysed turned out to be erudite essays on abstruse classical or similar subjects. Myers' collaborators in this project were Edmund Gurney, who died in 1888 and Henry Sidgwick (died 1900) and they worked through several automatic writing mediums, most of whom had no knowledge of the subjects transmitted. This material has been published in great detail across many volumes of the <u>Proceedings of the Society for Psychical Research</u> and has also been summarised in the following book:

Saltmarsh, H.F. **(1938)** *Evidence of Personal Survival from Cross Correspondences* **Bell London**

However, simpler accounts of the cross correspondences can be found in Ellison (1988), Brookesmith (1989), Iverson (1992) – see Section 1 above – and in many other general accounts of psychical research. This research provides some of the best evidence for survival of death yet available. As Ellison states when considering alternative explanations for this enormous amount of evidence: "I choose the survival hypothesis."; and, in this, he is much more positive in his response than is Saltmarsh. David Lorimer has summed up this body of evidence as follows: "Designed to prove the survival of collaborative intelligence, this is evidence of the most persuasive nature that would impress all but the most fanatical sceptic."

At the turn of the 20th century a book was published which has been recognised as an indisputable masterpiece, being an ambitious attempt to review the strange powers of the human mind. Colin Wilson describes it as "…probably the most comprehensive work ever written on the subject of the paranormal." F.W.H. Myers (1843-1901) undertook meticulous research for almost 30 years and his *Human Personality and its Survival of Bodily Death* was the result of an enormous amount of work covering all aspects of psychic phenomena. The book was over 1300 pages long and divided into two volumes; it was published in 1903, two years after Myers' untimely death.

Myers, F.W.H. **(1903)** *Human Personality and its Survival of Bodily Death* **Longmans Green London** An abridged version in one volume, leaving out much of the detailed case histories, was published 1919. **The abridged version has been reprinted by Pilgrim Books Norwich UK (1992) ISBN 0-946259-39-9** This latest printing contains the unabridged Epilogue from the original edition.

James H. Hyslop (1854-1920) was Professor of Logic and Ethics at Columbia University, New York from 1889 to 1902 and became one of the most distinguished American psychical researchers. Initially very sceptical, his investigation of the medium Mrs. Piper – and particularly the wealth of personal information he received from her – convinced him of the reality of survival. He went on to become a prolific researcher and the founding father of the American Society for Psychical Research. He wrote several books on psychical research and particularly on survival.

These are, in their British editions:

Hyslop, James H. (1906) *Science and a Future Life* **Putnam London**

Hyslop, James H. (1906) *Enigmas of Psychical Research* **Putnam London**

Hyslop, James H. (1908) *Psychical Research and the Resurrection* **Fisher Unwin London**

Hyslop, James H. (1913) *Psychical Research and Survival* **Bell & Sons London**

Hyslop, James H. (1919) *Borderland of Psychical Research* **Werner Laurie London**

Hyslop, James H. (1919) *Contact With the Other World* **Werner Laurie London**

Camille Flammarion (1842-1925) was a leading French astronomer of his time and an author of many popular books on astronomy. Later in life he also became involved in psychical research, writing extensively on this subject. As Sylvia Wright in her book *When Spirits Come Calling* (see p 91) states: "During the early part of the 20th century a distinguished French astronomer, Camille Flammarion, authored a series of books on paranormal phenomena. Encouraged by his interest in the subject, over the course of half a century, thousands of people from around the world wrote to him about their uncanny experiences – which often involved contact with the dead. His three volume study, *Death and Its Mystery*, comprised extensive quotes from hundreds of their letters, many of them accompanied by confirming letters from other witnesses to the events involved. In his concluding chapter, he observed:

> "The object of this work has been attained…The occurrences cited, the truth of which has been duly established, prove that there is no death…"Death is the portal of life". The body is but an organic garment of the spirit; it dies, it changes, it disintegrates: the spirit remains… The universe is a dynamism. An intelligent force rules all. The soul cannot be destroyed".

Professor Flammarion became President of the Society for Psychical Research in 1923. His classic work, *Death and Its Mystery*, was published in three parts over a period of time:

Flammarion, Camille (1909) *Death and Its Mystery. Proofs of the existence of the soul* Fisher Unwin London

Flammarion, Camille (1923) *Death and Its Mystery. Manifestations and apparitions of the dead* Fisher Unwin London

Flammarion, Camille (1923) *Death and Its Mystery. The soul after death* Fisher Unwin London

Charles Richet (1850-1935) was a French professor of physiology, an impeccable researcher and winner of the 1913 Nobel Prize for medicine. He also spent many years of his professional career investigating all aspects of parapsychology both on his own and in cooperation with other well-known investigators. This latter part of his work was recorded in one of the classics of this field of research.

Richet, C. (1923) *Thirty Years of Psychical Research. Being a treatise on metapsychics* Collins & Sons London 2nd edition translated by S. DeBrath

In a book of nearly 650 pages, Professor Richet describes an enormous volume of research, the results of which – almost against his will – he had to accept as proof of the reality of psychic phenomena. Starting off as a complete sceptic he was slowly convinced by the mounting weight of reliable evidence of the reality of different aspects of ESP: telepathy, clairvoyance and precognition, and also of psychokinesis. With particular difficulty, because it went against all his physiological training and experience, he also eventually accepted ectoplasmic materialisation as a reality. As he stated (pp 543-544):

> "There is ample proof that experimental materialization (ectoplasmic) should take definite rank as a scientific fact. Assuredly we do not understand it. It is very absurd, if a truth can be absurd.

> "Spiritualists have blamed me for using this word "absurd"; and have not been able to understand that to admit the reality of these phenomena was to me an actual pain; but to ask a physiologist, a physicist, or a chemist to admit that a form that has a circulation of blood, warmth, and muscles, that exhales carbonic acid, has weight, speaks, and thinks, can issue from a human body is to ask of him an intellectual effort that is really painful.

> "Yes it is absurd; but no matter – it is true."

However, at the time of the publication of his book he couldn't bring himself to admit to the reality of survival, or what he called "the spiritist hypothesis".

Baron Albert von Schrenck Notzing (1862-1929) was a German aristocrat and practising physician whose private wealth gave him the means to undertake an extensive programme of psychical research. He concentrated on physical phenomena, particularly on ectoplasmic materialisations, and his carefully controlled experimental techniques put his results beyond all reasonable criticism. He worked with the well-known materialisation mediums of the time, Eusapia Palladino, 'Eva C.' and the Schneider brothers. His description of his work remains the most detailed account of the experiments of the time, and was published as:

Schrenck Notzing, Baron Albert von (1920) *Phenomena of Materialisation. A contribution to the investigation of mediumistic teleplastics* **Kegan Paul Trench Trubner & Co. London.** Translated E.E. Fournier d'Albe. First published 1914 as *Materialisations – phaenomene* Reinhardt Munich Germany

This book, together with those of Juliette Bisson and Gustave Geley, form the most detailed evidence available for the reality of ectoplasmic materialised forms. See also:

Bisson, Juliette A. (1914) *Les Phenomenes de Materialisation* **Librairie Felix Alcan Paris France**

Geley, Gustave (1927) *Clairvoyance and Materialisation* First published [French] in Paris (1924) **Republished (1975) Arno Press London ISBN 0-405-07020-9**

Glen Hamilton. In 1921 a well-known doctor and parliamentarian from Winnipeg, Canada called Glen Hamilton became interested in psychical research. He and a group of like-minded friends set up a series of experimental séances with some gifted local mediums and, over a period of more than ten years, produced a wide range of psychic phenomena. Dr Hamilton worked under strictly controlled conditions and, using specialised equipment such as a bank of different types of cameras to record events, produced some remarkable results. In particular, they recorded more than 60 "teleplasms" or materialisations, many of which showed specific pictures of recognisable faces or particular human forms or structures, thus supporting the findings of Professor Richet. Dr Hamilton believed that through the 'teleplasms'

produced by the mediums "transcendental intelligences" were able to make contact with this world. His researches are described in:

Hamilton, T. Glen (1942) *Intention and Survival. Psychical research and the bearing of intentional actions by trance personalities on the problem of human survival* The Macmillan Company of Canada Toronto. Second edition edited by Margaret L. Hamilton (1977) Regency Press London

Apparitions

Apparitions are an important source of evidence supporting the concept of survival. They have been recorded from ancient times in almost all cultures and are a common form of psychic experience. They can be classified into three categories: apparitions of the living, where an individual sees an apparition of another living person – the latter often being physically separated from the viewer's position by considerable distances; apparitions of the dying, where someone sees the appearance of an individual elsewhere who is on the point of, or close to, death; and apparitions of the dead, where people who may have been dead for days, months or years become visible to the percipient. An apparition is usually seen as a true representation of the individual concerned – a three-dimensional, apparently solid body clothed in the manner expected by the percipient and in all ways appearing to be a normal person but which can appear and disappear suddenly, often by passing through a wall or door. It may seek to communicate with the viewer, by gesticulations or by speaking a few words. They may appear in daylight (over 40%), in good artificial light (10-20%), or in darkness.

The earliest systematic investigations of apparitions were initiated by the SPR and published as *Phantasms of the Living* and the *Census of Hallucinations.* Thereafter, numerous studies of apparitions have been undertaken in Britain, France, Italy, Germany, America and many other countries, providing an enormous archive of information on the subject. In spite of this large amount of material supporting the validity of apparitions, the fact that a large proportion of the cases are only seen by a single viewer has resulted in sceptics 'writing off' this phenomenon. They maintained that they are simply cases of hallucinations occurring purely in the minds of the individuals concerned, however well these cases may have been observed and reported. Accordingly, they have no objective reality of their own. However, there are a significant number of cases where two or more individuals have seen the same apparition, viewing it from different angles. Since hallucinations are purely subjective – being a mental process only 'visible' to the hallucinator – then such apparitions cannot be hallucinations and must have some objective reality.

Some of the more important books or reports concerning apparitions are:

Gurney, E., Myers, F.W.H. and Podmore, F. (1886) *Phantasms of the Living* **Trubner & Co. London,** two volumes. Abridged version in one volume edited by Mrs Sidgwick published (1918)

One of the earliest major publications of the SPR, these volumes contain several hundred cases, obtained by questioning 5,700 people, almost exclusively dealing with apparitions of living persons seen by other living persons. This was followed up several years later by:

Sidgwick, H., Myers, F.W.H., Podmore, F. and Johnson, Alice (1894) *Report on the Census of Hallucinations* **Proceedings of the Society for Psychical Research, vol 10 pp 25-422**

The Census of Hallucinations was the result of questioning 17,000 persons and consisted of reports of 352 apparitions of living people and 163 of dead people. This response showed that almost 10% of those questioned had had sensory hallucinations of the type described in the question.

Bennett, Sir Ernest (1939) *Apparitions and Haunted Houses. A survey of evidence* **Faber and Faber London**

Bennett's extensive review of apparitions (104 cases) was drawn from two sources. First from the very large archive of reports found in the *Proceedings* and *Journal* of the Society for Psychical Research and, second, from material sent in to him by respondents to a broadcast appeal for personal experiences. In both sections he only included those cases which had the highest evidential value; many of the reports were of 'collective cases' where two or more individuals had witnessed the events recorded. He suggests three hypotheses which might explain these phenomena:

  1 That they are purely subjective hallucinations;

  2 that the apparitions are objective entities existing separately in space; and,

  3 that apparitions occur by telepathy between, for example, the dead and the individuals aware of them. Bennett's preferred explanation is the third, telepathy, hypothesis.

Tyrrell, G.N.M. (1942) *Apparitions* **Gerald Duckworth London. Also published (1953) Pantheon Books New York USA**

A valuable analysis of our understanding of apparitions in the mid-20th century. Tyrrell divides apparitions into four categories: experimental – those of living people where the agent has deliberately tried to make his apparition visible to a particular percipient; crisis-apparitions – particularly death and near-death – where the individual represented by the apparition is undergoing some crisis; post-mortem purposeful contact (post-mortem cases), where enough time has elapsed following the death of the individual concerned for crisis causation to be ruled out; and hauntings of place, where apparitions (ghosts) habitually haunt certain places.

Hart, Hornell (1956) *Six Theories about Apparitions: a co-operative report with associated collaborators in the International Project for Research on ESP Projection* Proceedings of the Society for Psychical Research **vol 50 pp 153-239**

Following an international conference in Utrecht in 1953, Professor Hart organised a team of 48 collaborators from 12 countries to assess the evidence associated with apparitions and to consider the possible theories explaining this phenomenon. The report published in 1956 concluded strongly in favour of survival as the most likely explanation for apparitions.

MacKenzie, Andrew (1971) *Apparitions and Ghosts. A modern study* **Arthur Barker Ltd. London SBN 213-00291-4**

Andrew Mackenzie presents a series of forty nine cases of apparitions carefully selected from a wide range of material offered to him following appeals to the public. All the cases were new and include examples of every type of apparition. Care was taken to ensure that each case was well substantiated and was not easily explicable by normal mechanisms; however, the material published was of varying quality. Although the author discusses his cases in the context of earlier studies, he did not come to any specific conclusions, leaving readers to draw their own.

Moody, Raymond A. with Perry, Paul (1993) *Reunions. Visionary encounters with departed loved ones* **Villard Books NY USA. Republished (1994) Little Brown & Co. London and (1995) Warner Books London ISBN 0-7515-1407-1**

Dr Moody, one of the pioneers of research into near-death experiences, investigates in this book a related phenomenon – the ancient art of mirror gazing. He reviews the history of the subject, the ability to see visions or apparitions of dead relatives, and then goes on to describe his own work in reconstructing – and using – a psychomanteum, a special chamber which can be used to facilitate visionary encounters with the departed. He describes many of the results he obtained by preparing individuals for this encounter and then allowing them to experience the effects of the psychomanteum. Many of those involved saw apparitions that convinced them that they had been in contact with dead relatives. Although some of the experiences can best be explained as material arising from the subconscious of the individual concerned, others are almost certainly direct, conscious encounters with the dead in which information was shared between the experiencer and the apparition.

Valuable discussion and analysis of the subject of apparitions can also be found in the relevant chapters in Hart (1959), Almeder (1992) and Becker (1993) (see pp 8-9).

Proxy Sittings

A type of research called proxy sittings was developed in order to overcome the suggestion that, when people consulted mediums in order to obtain information about relatives who had died, the medium's subconscious picked up information by telepathy from the sitter, and this was embroidered and recycled by the medium. This criticism was overcome by sending 'proxy sitters' to the medium who knew nothing about the individuals concerned, the deceased and the person wishing to communicate, only their names. Possibly the best example of this work is that undertaken by the Rev. Charles Drayton Thomas using the medium Mrs. Osborne Leonard. For more than 20 years he had over 500 sittings with Mrs. Leonard collecting proxy information about deceased people. Much of the detail of the communications was later confirmed by the relatives concerned. The Drayton Thomas/Osborne Leonard partnership produced a great deal of evidence supporting survival – not only proxy sittings but also word association tests, book tests and newspaper tests – and the only possible criticism that could be made against this work is that of fraud. Nobody has been able to extend this criticism to these proxy sittings, successfully. The Rev. Drayton Thomas' research has been recorded in the Proceedings of the Society for Psychical Research, but he also wrote several books, three of which are:

Thomas, Charles Drayton (1922) *Some New Evidence for Human Survival* **Collins London**

Thomas, Charles Drayton (1928) *Life Beyond Death with Evidence* **W. Collins Sons & Co. Ltd. London**

Thomas, Charles Drayton (1936) *An Amazing Experiment* **Lectures Universal London**

A very useful summary of Drayton Thomas' work is given in Chapter 6 of Professor Hornell Hart's *The Enigma of Survival* (See page 8).

Gauld, Alan (1982) *Mediumship and Survival. A century of investigations* Heinemann London SBN 434-28320-7 Series editor Brian Inglis. Published on behalf of the Society for Psychical Research (SPR) New impression published (1983) Paladin London ISBN 0-586-08429-0

Mediumship and Survival was published to celebrate the centenary of the SPR. It is a thorough review of the whole range of research undertaken by the Society during its first 100 years. Gauld provides a detailed and balanced assessment of all aspects of the Society's work which is carefully, even cautiously, stated. Although he does not specifically affirm his acceptance of the survival hypothesis, it is clear that he considers the anti-survival case to be often flawed. In particular, he draws attention to the weaknesses of the Super-psi [the preferred expression to Super-ESP] hypothesis as a satisfactory explanation for mediumistic phenomena. He considers that much more research is needed before any firm conclusions can be drawn on the case for survival. An important contribution to the literature – but one which is not always an easy read.

The Electronic Voice Phenomenon

A more recently discovered technique for seeking to communicate with discarnate spirits has been called Electronic Voice Phenomenon (EVP). Using this technique investigators have been able to record 'paranormal' voices on tape recorders or similar equipment – voices which cannot be heard when the instrument is recording but which can be heard when the tape is played back. Major advantages of this technique are that it uses standard tape recorders and tapes, rather than a human medium, and also that it can be controlled and duplicated under laboratory conditions.

The American inventor Thomas Edison was the first person to attempt to make contact with 'the other side' using sensitive instrumentation during the 1920s. However he died before he achieved any success and it wasn't until 1959 that the first such results were obtained by the Swede Friedrich Jurgenson. After several years of work Jurgenson published his results in:

Jurgenson, Friedrich (1964) *Voices from the Universe* [publisher unknown]

This research was taken up by scientists such as Professor Hans Bender in Germany and Dr Konstatin Raudive from Latvia. Dr Raudive and two colleagues produced more than 100,000 tapes under strict laboratory conditions. This material was written up as:

Raudive, Konstatin (1971) *Breakthrough; An amazing experiment in electronic communication with the dead* Colin Smyth London SBN 900675-543 Translated from the original German edition published (1971) Also published (1971) as *Breakthrough: Electronic communication with the dead may be possible* Zebra Books New York USA

Other books dealing with EVP are:

Bander, Peter (1973) *Voices from the Tapes* Drake New York USA ISBN 0-887494-47-9

Villencia, Jeff (1988) *Echoes from Eternity* Inner Light Publications New Brunswick NJ USA

Connelly, Gerry (1995) *The Afterlife for the Atheist* Domra Publications Corby UK

A recently published book which provides a readable summary of this phenomenon is:

Chisholm, Judith (2000) *Voices from the Dead. How the dead talk to us* Jon Carpenter Publishing Charlbury Oxford UK ISBN 1-897766-59-9

In this book the author describes how she came to be convinced of the survival of her son, who died unexpectedly, through the medium of EVP; and also describes the history of the development of the phenomenon together with an outline of how the procedure works.

Instrumental Trans-communication

A development of EVP from about 1980 is what is termed Instrumental Trans-communication (ITC). In this investigators use a wide range of equipment – telephones, radios, televisions, answering machines, faxes and computers – to establish contact with the dead. These results are often highly evidential with the ability to maintain conversations with, and even to obtain pictures – on TV – of relatives and others who have died. Three books describing much of this work are:

Rogo, D. Scott and Bayless, Raymond (1979) *Phone Calls from the Dead* New English Library London

Fuller, John G. (1985) *The Ghost of 29 Megacycles* Souvenir Press London ISBN 0-285-62691-4 Also published (1987) Grafton Books London

Kubis, Pat and Macy, Mark (1995) *Conversations Beyond the Light. Communications with departed friends and colleagues by electronic means* **Griffin Publishing/Continuing Life Research Boulder Colorado USA ISBN 1-882180-47-X**

This relatively recent book is of particular value in that it contains, amongst much other material, a chapter on "Getting Started" with ITC and a section of evidential material – pictures of 'dead' people transmitted from the other side of death via video and computer generated images.

Useful reviews of EVP can be found in Brookesmith and Zammit (pp 2 and 10 respectively, above) and of ITC in Zammit. Although, as with much mediumistic communication, some of the results from these techniques are both trivial and can possibly be being derived from the subconscious minds of the operators/sitters, there has nevertheless been a great deal of highly evidential material produced by these techniques which supports survival.

The Scole Report

One of the most recent and comprehensive investigations into survival is that which was undertaken during the 1990s, mainly at Scole in Norfolk, and which has been called The Scole Report. The research involved three groups of individuals:

> 1 The Scole group, a mediumistic group the core of which consisted of four individuals, Robin and Sandra Foy and another husband and wife team, around which all the reported phenomena were associated;

> 2 the investigators, three senior and experienced members of the Society for Psychical Research, Montague Keen, Arthur Ellison and David Fontana;

> 3 the spirit team, a group of discarnate spirit guides who communicated through the entranced mediums.

Under carefully controlled conditions a variety of phenomena, often of a remarkable nature, were recorded. Among these were displays of moving lights; the production of spirit forms and shapes; the imposition of a wide variety of images on sealed films; apports and electronic voice phenomena.

All this material has been methodically recorded by the investigators in more than 300 pages of the Proceedings of the Society for Psychical Research, thus:

Keen, Montague, Ellison, Arthur and Fontana, David (1999) *The Scole Report. An account of an investigation into the genuineness of a range of physical phenomena associated with a mediumistic group in Norfolk England* **Proceedings of the Society for Psychical Research vol 58 part 220** (November 1999)

The report is very heavy going, being a detailed scientific review and assessment of very complex phenomena. The Abstract, in a typically scientifically objective way, summarises the project as follows:

"This report is the outcome of a three-year investigation of a Group claiming to receive both messages and materialised or physical objects from a number of collaborative spirit communicators. It has been conducted principally by three senior members of the Society for Psychical Research. In the course of over 20 sittings the investigators were unable to detect any direct indication of fraud or deception, and encountered evidence favouring the hypothesis of intelligent forces, whether originating in the human psyche or from discarnate sources, able to influence material objects, and to convey associated meaningful messages, both visual and aural."

NB This abstract summarises the conclusions of the three individual authors; the Society for Psychical Research does not necessarily endorse these findings. See the disclaimer printed in the Acknowledgements, page ix.

On the other hand the Scole phenomena have also been written up in a much more readable form as:

Solomon, Grant and Jane (1999) *The Scole Experiment. Scientific evidence for life after death* **Judy Piatkus (Publishers) Ltd. London ISBN 0-7499-2032-7** [Paperback] **published (2000) ISBN 0-7499-2105-6**

This book describes the experiments undertaken at Scole in a more down-to-earth and 'popular' way. The authors are writers who view the experiments from the point of view of interested outsiders.

The best assessment of the Scole phenomena is probably obtained by reading and comparing both accounts. In spite of the reticence of the SPR Report, it is clear that a remarkable range of phenomena were witnessed over many experimental sessions and that the most likely explanation for the observations was that they were generated by a cooperative effort between the Scole group and a team of discarnate spirit entities.

A very interesting and enlightening summary of what happened during and after the Scole experiment is contained in two reports published in the journal of the Scientific and Medical Network. The Network is an informal, international group of scientists, doctors and others who question "...the assumptions of contemporary scientific and medical thinking, so often limited by exclusively materialistic reasoning". In the first of these reports Montague Keen, one of the original investigators, gives his own personal analysis of what occurred. His conclusions are that the phenomena were real and not subject to fraud, and were the result of actual interactions between the Scole group and a team of spirit communicators:

Keen, Montague (2000) *The Scole Event.* **The Scientific & Medical Network Review No 73 (August 2000) pp 11-14 ISSN 1362-1211**

In the second report, Crawford Knox analyses the responses of many critics of the Scole experiment – not least some members of the Society for Psychical Research. Knox is particularly critical of the sceptics who are unable open-mindedly to look at any evidence for survival but adhere rigidly to the materialist explanation for everything in the universe. As Knox states: " ...the assumption that the world is entirely material and everything can be explained within a closed materialist framework has passed its sell-by date. It is difficult to reconcile with quantum physics and it involves ignoring or explaining away an entire range of mental and spiritual experiences, including the very consciousness from which the materialist picture is built":

Knox, Crawford (2000) *The Scole Report. Some implications for parapsychology* **The Scientific & Medical Network Review** No 73 (August 2000) pp 14-17 **ISSN 1362-1211**

The Afterlife Experiments

Another recent, and highly significant, series of experiments has been that undertaken by Professor Gary Schwartz and his colleague Dr Linda Russek in America. These two investigators set out in the late 1990s to test several of the most prominent US mediums in an attempt to demonstrate that mediumistic communications actually did originate from discarnate souls. They developed a series of experiments, with each successive one being refined so as to overcome the potential shortcomings and criticisms that could be levelled at those which went before. The results that they obtained were quite phenomenal, with very high levels of correctly positive information being "brought through" by the mediums concerning a series of sitters with whom they had had no contact, either previously or during the experiments. Starting off as a convinced sceptic, Dr Schwartz eventually became convinced by the validity of the results that the human soul does survive death and that communication between the physical and spiritual planes is possible.

Very well written, this book provides not only an account of their work which is easily comprehensible by the ordinary reader but also reprints the manuscripts of several published papers giving the scientific details of the research for those wishing to know more. Dr Schwartz discusses how a wider awareness of survival would impact on our lives and how this might change humanity. He also devotes two chapters to possible fraud in this type of research and to countering the charges of the 'professional sceptics' who remain unconvinced by even the best work. The details of the book are:

Schwartz, Gary E. with Simon, William L. (2002) *The Afterlife Experiments. Breakthrough scientific evidence of life after death* **Pocket Books New York USA ISBN 0-7434-3658-X**

3 Indirect Research
Important Research Providing Indirect Support for Survival

As well as the direct research noted above, there is also a considerable amount of work which provides strong support for the concept of survival, although it was not undertaken with the specific intention of demonstrating that survival is (or is not) a reality. We will consider here three lines of work which fall into this category:

(a) Reincarnation research;

(b) Research into Out of the Body and Near Death Experiences; and

(c) Research into Past-Life Regression.

(a) Reincarnation Research

A belief in the idea of reincarnation has been, and is, widely held across the world. Although a belief in this concept is usually considered only to be associated with that area of Southeast Asia where Hinduism and Buddhism are the major religions, in reality it is much more widespread than this. It can be found, for example, among the Shiite Moslems of Western Asia, the inhabitants of West and East Africa, the tribal people of parts of North America and a considerable proportion of the population of Brazil – as well as numerous other groups of people across the globe. A belief in reincarnation is also steadily increasing in the West.

The concept of reincarnation or rebirth is directly related to the idea of the survival of death in that, depending on the different religious or philosophical systems which hold this belief, some aspect of the original individual has to continue through death and eventually be reborn in a new body as a new individual. The entity which survives death and is reborn as a new personality carries with it the good and bad 'karma' of the original person.

There are many books available which cover various aspects of the subject of reincarnation, several of which are suggested here for general reading and understanding of the subject. These are:

Head, Joseph and Cranston, Sylvia (1977) *Reincarnation. The Phoenix Fire Mystery. An East-West dialogue on death and rebirth from the worlds of religion, science, psychology, philosophy, art and literature, and from great thinkers of the past and present* **Theosophical University Press Pasadena CA USA ISBN 1-55700-026-3** Recently reissued [paperback] as:

Cranston, Sylvia (1998) *Reincarnation. The Phoenix Fire Mystery* Theosophical University Press Pasadena CA USA ISBN 1-55700-026-3

As suggested in the subtitle, this book is an extensive and detailed (620 pp) review of the concept of reincarnation, moving from antiquity to modern times and quoting material from all aspects of religion, culture and science. It is encyclopaedic in its coverage but very readable and informative.

Cerminara, Gina (1967) *Many Mansions* Neville Spearman London

Many Mansions is a straightforward interpretation of the spiritual philosophy behind the concept of reincarnation, based on Edgar Cayce's work (see p 64).

Hall, Judy (2001) *Way of Reincarnation* Thorsons London ISBN 0-00-710290-9

A very recent, straightforward, introductory text on the subject of reincarnation. Although not as detailed as the other books included here, it covers most aspects of the subject in a way which is helpful to those wishing to explore the subject for the first time.

Fisher, Joe (1993) *The Case For Reincarnation* Diamond Books London ISBN 0-261-66029-2 First published in Britain (1985) Granada Publishing

In the foreword to the book the author states that evidence in support of the case for reincarnation has been drawn from "empirical research, medical assessment, spiritual wisdom, metaphysical investigation, historical record, mystical perception and wide-ranging contemporary experience". *The Case for Reincarnation* covers all these areas and also provides an extensive bibliography for further reading.

Hardo, Trutz (2001) *Children Who Have Lived Before. Reincarnation today* C.W. Daniel Saffron Walden Essex UK ISBN 0-85207-352-6

Trutz Hardo, described as "the most well known expert on reincarnation and regression therapy in Germany", has produced a very readable account of the evidence for reincarnation as evidenced in the widespread reports of children's cases from across the world. The material is reported as a series of summaries of cases from other researchers, particularly those of Professor Ian Stevenson, interspersed with his own commentary. Written by someone who is convinced of the reality of reincarnation, the book is essentially a descriptive, rather than a critical, review of the subject. The last chapter, "Reincarnation in the light of a new world view", describes how both personal and society's views of life might change dramatically if a belief in reincarnation became widely accepted.

Fenwick, Peter and Fenwick, Elisabeth (1999) *Past Lives. An investigation into reincarnation memories* Headline Book Publishing London ISBN 0-7472-1841-2

A good, up-to-date review of the subject of reincarnation written by authors with considerable experience in this field. The book re-examines many of the most interesting and best attested cases on record and also analyses more than a hundred first-hand British accounts given to the authors by people who believe that they have memories of a past life. The Fenwicks discuss how far a Western scientific framework can explain these memories and where we might look for answers outside such a framework.

Although the concept of reincarnation has been considered by Western philosophers for at least two centuries, it is only fairly recently that it has become more widely understood by ordinary people. One of the earliest, well publicised cases of an individual who was investigated for having claimed to remember details of her most recent life was that of Shanti Devi, an eight year old Indian girl born in Delhi who in 1935 claimed to be the reincarnation of a housewife who had died in childbirth in a small northern Indian town. In this, classic, case (described by Jeffrey Iverson on p 4), Shanti Devi provided extensive detailed evidence – which she could not have known by normal means – about her previous family, none of which was shown to be false or mistaken. Cases like this led on to wide-ranging research during the second half of the last century. The leading figure in this field over the past 40 years has been **Dr Ian Stevenson**, Professor of Psychiatry at the University of Virginia, who has studied more than 2600 cases from all parts of the world and who has published his results in many scientific papers and several books. The quality of evidence in favour of reincarnation varies considerably from case to case, but Dr Stevenson's detailed and painstaking research has built up a compelling dossier of material in favour of reincarnation. As Iverson has stated: "Dr Stevenson considers fraud, hallucination and telepathy as options in every investigation. But the kernel of his work is the twenty-five cases he believes are so strong that reincarnation is the most logical explanation". Some of the key publications (books) produced by Dr Stevenson are:

Stevenson, Ian (1966) *Twenty Cases Suggestive of Reincarnation* <u>Proceedings of the American Society for Psychical Research</u>, vol XXVI (September 1966) American Society for Psychical Research New York USA [Reprinted as:]

Stevenson, Ian (1974) *Twenty Cases Suggestive of Reincarnation* 2nd rev ed University Press of Virginia Charlottesville VA USA ISBN 0-8139-0546-X

Stevenson, Ian (1975) *Cases of the Reincarnation Type* vol 1 *Ten Cases in India* University Press of Virginia Charlottesville ISBN 0-8139-0602-4

Stevenson, Ian (1977) *Cases of the Reincarnation Type* vol 2 *Ten cases in Sri Lanka* University Press of Virginia Charlottesville ISBN 0-8139-0624-5

Stevenson, Ian (1980) *Cases of the Reincarnation Type* vol 3 *Twelve cases in Lebanon and Turkey* University Press of Virginia Charlottesville ISBN 0-8139-0816-7

Stevenson, Ian (1983) *Cases of the Reincarnation Type* vol 4 *Twelve cases in Thailand and Burma* University Press of Virginia Charlottesville ISBN 0-8139-0960-0

Stevenson, Ian (1987) *Children Who Remember Previous Lives. A question of reincarnation* University Press of Virginia Charlottesville ISBN 0-8139-1140-0

This is probably the best scientifically argued account of the case for reincarnation.

Stevenson, Ian (1997) *Where Reincarnation and Biology Intersect* Praeger Publishers Westport & London [paperback] ISBN 0-275-95189-8

This last book is particularly interesting as it deals with evidence for reincarnation which is based on physical manifestations, such as birth marks, that have been found to relate to experiences (often violent) remembered from a past life. It is a condensed and simplified version of a previously published two volume, medical monograph entitled *Reincarnation and Biology: A Contribution to the Etiology of Birthmarks and Birth Defects,* also published by Praeger (1997) ISBN 0-275-95282-7

Stevenson's books are generally of an academic nature, being written largely for professionals and scholars. As such many of them are often not easy reading for a wider audience. Probably the most straightforward of his publications, and the nearest to a 'popular read', are *Children Who Remember Previous Lives* and *Where Reincarnation and Biology Intersect.*

However, some of Professor Stevenson's work has been recorded in a very readable form in:

Schroder, Tom (1999) *Old Souls. The scientific evidence for past lives* Simon & Schuster New York USA ISBN 0-684-85192-X

Schroder, a sceptical journalist, persuaded Professor Stevenson to allow him to take part in the latter's field work in Lebanon, India and the American South. *Old Souls* consists of accounts of many case studies of children who clearly remembered details of their immediately previous life, providing evidence which convinced the author of the reality of reincarnation.

આ

Xenoglossy

There are many records of individuals, children or adults, who are able to speak and/or write a foreign language with which they have had no apparent previous contact or knowledge. Such cases are known as examples of xenoglossy. This phenomenon may happen spontaneously, when perhaps a child will suddenly begin to speak an unknown language, but more often it occurs when the individual is under hypnosis or in an altered state of consciousness. These cases may vary in extent from the use of a few words or sentences to total fluency in another language. The phenomenon of xenoglossy has been reviewed by Zammit (see p 10) and at greater length by Stevenson in his book *Xenoglossy* quoted below. Once all other explanations for such cases have been carefully excluded by research, there are only two ways in which they can be explained; either the language was learnt in a previous life and then recalled (reincarnation), or the knowledge is being imparted to the individual by a discarnate spirit. Whichever is the correct explanation such cases provide direct evidence for survival. Professor Stevenson's book is:

Stevenson, Ian (1974) *Xenoglossy. A review and report of a case* John Wright Bristol UK ISBN 0-7236-0347-2

In it he firstly reviews all the published reports on this subject and then describes the extensive and detailed investigation of the subject – a 37 year old American woman – who, under hypnosis, manifested a complete change of character. This different personality was that of a male who spoke fluent Swedish, whilst the original subject had no knowledge or apparent access to this language. Several years of study of this case led Stevenson to conclude that: "…it provides important evidence of the survival of human personality after death."; and, again, that it: "…offers strong evidence of the survival of physical death by some aspect of human personality." A more recent review of two well documented cases of xenoglossy can be found in:

Stevenson, Ian (1984) *Unlearned Language: New studies in xenoglossy* University Press of Virginia Charlottesville VA USA

"In this book Stevenson explores two of the most interesting and well documented cases on record: Dolores Jay, who under hypnosis manifested as 'Gretchen', a German speaking personality, and Uttara Haddur, who over a fifteen year period of her life, was repeatedly taken over by the personality of 'Sharada' a young 19th Century Bengali – and Bengali speaking – woman". (Elisabeth Fenwick).

☙

(b) Research into Out-of-the-Body and Near-Death Experiences

(i) The Out-of-the-Body Experience

The Out-of-the-Body Experience (OBE) is a widely reported phenomenon for which there is an extensive literature, describing not only what is reported to occur but also techniques by which individuals can learn to voluntarily undertake this experience. In an OBE the individual's consciousness, together with the invisible duplicate (astral) body, is apparently able to leave the physical body whilst retaining full awareness. The physical body then remains in deep sleep or unconsciousness whilst the person is able to travel wherever he or she wishes. Strange as this phenomenon may seem there is ample evidence that it can and does occur, particularly from the research by governments into "remote viewing", a technique used by military intelligence to obtain information from important sites which would otherwise be totally inaccessible. A study of OBEs clearly demonstrates that human consciousness is more than a product of the activity of the physical brain and that this greater reality (the human soul?) is able to survive the process of physical death. This subject has been reviewed in some detail by Zammit (see p 10)

Several investigators have undertaken studies of the OBE experience, either from extensive personal experience or by collecting and analysing the experiences of others. The published accounts of some of the best known of such investigators are listed here.

Sylvan Muldoon was a young American who, at the age of 12, began to have extensive experiences of OBEs which continued over many years. Eventually he contacted the well known psychical researcher, **Hereward Carrington**, and they collaborated to publish three books which described his experiences, detailed techniques that Muldoon had perfected by which others could experience OBEs and listed numerous case histories of experiences that they had collected from various sources. All this material appears in the following:

Muldoon, Sylvan J. and Carrington, Hereward (1992) *The Projection of the Astral Body* **Rider London ISBN 0-712-62582-8** First published (1929) and reissued in three editions and several impressions (1950) onwards, all by Rider. Also published (1970) Samuel Weiser NY USA

Muldoon's first book is one of the classics, possibly *the* classic, of modern literature on OBEs. As Hereward Carrington describes in his extended introduction, it is by no means the first book covering this subject but it is the first to describe the techniques and experiences in detail.

Muldoon, Sylvan J. (1935) *The Case for Astral Projection* **Aries Press Chicago USA**

Muldoon, Sylvan J. and Carrington, Hereward (1969) *The Phenomena of Astral Projection* **Rider London ISBN 0-090-38372-9** First published (1951) Rider. **Also published (1970) Samuel Weiser NY USA**

This was the first major collection of OBEs, obtained from a variety of sources including instances reported directly to the authors. They classified individual accounts into a number of categories according to their cause or triggering event.

Dr Robert Crookall was a senior scientist in the Geological Survey of Great Britain who, following retirement, dedicated himself to the study and publication of evidence supporting the case for survival and particularly the description and analysis of OBEs. In a series of books he presented hundreds of cases of OBEs which correlate very well with the material presented by Muldoon & Carrington. The relevant publications from his prolific output during the 1960s and 1970s are:

Crookall, R. (1961) *The Study and Practice of Astral Projection* **Aquarian Press London. Also published (1967) University Books NY USA**

Crookall, R. (1964) *More Astral Projections* **Aquarian Press London**

Crookall, R. (1964) *The Techniques of Astral Projection* **Aquarian Press London. Also published (1967) Darshana International Moradabad India**

Crookall, R. (1968) *The Mechanisms of Astral Projection* **Darshana International Moradabad India**

Crookall, R. (1972) *A Case Book of Astral Projections* **University Books NY USA**

Crookall, R. (1992) *Out of the Body Experiences. A fourth analysis* **Citadel Press NY USA ISBN 0-8065-1383-7** First published (1970) University Books NY USA ISBN 0-8065-0610-5 and also (1986) Citadel Press NY USA

A useful summary of Dr Crookall's views and research on OBEs is contained in:

Crookall, R. (1973) *Out-of-the-Body Experiences and Survival* **Chapter 5 pp 66-88 in Pearce-Higgins, J.D. and Whitby, G. Stanley (1973)** *Life, Death and Psychical Research. Studies on behalf of The Churches' Fellowship for Psychical and Spiritual Studies* **Rider London ISBN 0-09-115810-9**

Robert Monroe was a successful American businessman who, in 1958, unexpectedly began to have involuntary OBEs; an activity about which he was completely ignorant and for which he was totally unprepared. Initially unpredictable and uncontrollable, he eventually learned to control the process and set up a research group, which became The Monroe Institute, where the phenomenon of OBEs – both his own and those of other volunteers – could be fully explored. Since the 1960s Monroe has carried on this work through the Institute and he has written three books about his research and experiences in this field. In the first two of these he has recorded his OBEs and the discoveries he has made over thirty years; in the third, using his own and others' experiences, he describes wider and more extensive explorations into spiritual realities. The books are:

Monroe, R. A. (1971) *Journeys Out of the Body* **Doubleday New York USA ISBN 0-385-00861-9 Also published (1972) Souvenir Press London**

Monroe, R. A. (1985) *Far Journeys* **Doubleday New York USA ISBN 0-385-23181-4**

Monroe, R. A. (1994) *Ultimate Journey* **Doubleday New York USA ISBN 0-385-47207-2 Also published [paperback] (1998) Doubleday New York USA ISBN 0-385-47208-0**

Other books on this subject are:

Green, Celia (1968) *Out-of-the-Body Experiences* **Proceedings of the Institute of Psychophysical Research, vol II. Institute of Psychophysical Research Oxford**

This book is based on the material obtained from the large number of responses to an appeal made via the media for individuals who had had out-of-the-body experiences. The material consisted of the written narratives of the respondents together with their replies to two questionnaires. The data were then analysed in relation to a whole range of factors associated with the experiences, such as sex and age of subjects, triggering factors, number and duration of experiences, occurrence whether awake or asleep, etc. It is a useful and interesting descriptive study but one with little, if any, discussion or conclusions. The author coins a new term for OBEs – "ecsosomatic experiences".

࿐

Blackmore, Susan J. (1982) *Beyond the Body. An investigation of out-of-the-body experiences* **Heinemann London. Published on behalf of the Society for Psychical Research. Series editor Brian Inglis ISBN 0-434-07470-5**

Dr Blackmore has written a worthwhile and critical review of all aspects of out-of-the-body experiences, including the various collections of cases and the theories which have been put forward to account for the phenomenon. Although the author is sceptical towards the concept of survival, preferring more down-to-earth explanations for the OBE phenomenon, nevertheless she has brought together a great deal of useful information for the OBE student. It is a book which should be read in parallel with the classic descriptions of OBEs.

࿐

Two books which describe the American governmental involvement in paranormal research and particularly the work on remote viewing are:

Morehouse, D. A. (1996) *Psychic Warrior. The true story of the CIA's paranormal espionage program* **Michael Joseph London ISBN 0-7181-4178-4 First published (1996) St. Martin's Press USA**

This is a strange but remarkable book. David Morehouse was a young, high flying, US Army officer apparently destined for great things, who was accidentally wounded in the head whilst on manoeuvres in 1987. As a result of the injury he began to have uncontrolled visions and OBEs , and this newly developed faculty led him to be recruited for training and eventual work as a remote viewer for the CIA/Defense Intelligence Agency's secret programmes of "psychic spying". The book describes autobiographically his initial career, his training as a remote viewer and in considerable detail some of the work he undertook and the results obtained. In the second part it deals with how he became aware of the Agency's work on training people in "remote influencing" – teaching them to become offensive weapons – and, rebelling against this and becoming determined to expose what was an immoral programme, how he and his family endured the full force of the US Intelligence

39

community's attempts to silence him. He survived, and wrote *Psychic Warrior* as his exposé of what was, and probably still is, going on.

Schnabel, Jim (1997) *Remote Viewers. The secret history of America's psychic spies* Dell Publishing New York USA ISBN 0-4402-2306-7

(ii) The Near-Death Experience

A particular type of OBE, the Near-Death Experience (NDE), is especially relevant from the point of view of this bibliography since recent wide-ranging research into this phenomenon provides strong support for the concept of the survival of death. NDEs have been reported since early times but the development of improved medical resuscitation techniques in recent decades has meant that more and more people can be revived from the state of clinical death and are thus able to report their experiences during the period in which they had 'died'. NDEs are subjective experiences which usually follow on from serious illnesses, accidents or operations, although they may occur occasionally without such traumatic introductions. During an NDE the process described above occurs, with the fully conscious astral body leaving the physical body behind in an apparently dead condition. It then undergoes a series of events which are reported as the first stages of the afterlife. Not all NDEs follow the same pattern, but a full experience usually consists of a number of stages. Various researchers have described different numbers of these stages, the following is an outline of that described by **Dr Melvin Morse**:

1 The individual, having come to the crisis of his illness, realises that he has died – perhaps by hearing his death pronounced by a doctor.

2 He finds himself at peace and free of pain – he is released from the earlier bodily stress and turmoil.

3 An out of the body experience develops. He finds himself, perhaps, looking down on the hospital staff still struggling to resuscitate him.

4 Moving away from the death scene, he enters a long dark tunnel and rapidly moves towards a light shining at the end of the tunnel.

5 At the end of the tunnel, in a beautiful light filled environment, he is met and welcomed by a group of people among whom there are usually relatives who have predeceased him.

6 He is then met by a being of light, a being full of love, compassion and understanding.

7 This being, through non-verbal communication, leads him through an evaluation of his life, including a detailed panoramic playback of the events which had affected others.

8 He is 'told' by the being that he has to return to life on earth as there is more work to be done there. He may try to resist this but is involuntarily drawn back into his body and returns to normal consciousness.

9 In most cases this experience transforms his personality and he becomes, for example, more loving and caring and loses any fear of death.

The modern study of NDEs was essentially initiated by **Dr Raymond Moody** who first published the results of his pioneering work in 1975, although others, particularly Dr Elisabeth Kübler-Ross, [sometimes spelt Elizabeth] were also deeply involved in this field. Moody was followed by an increasing number of researchers who published books and reports during the 1980s and 1990s. Because of the importance of this subject in relation to the concept of survival, this literature is reviewed at some length.

Moody, Raymond A. (1975) *Life After Life* **Mockingbird Books New York USA. Also published (1976) Corgi edition ISBN 0-552-10316-0 and (1976) Bantam edition ISBN 0-553-10080-7**

A study of over 100 cases of NDEs. Republished as:

Moody, Raymond A. (1980) *Life After Life* **Bantam Books New York USA ISBN 0-553-14609-2**

Life After Life is a classic which has been published and republished in many editions. This was followed by a sequel:

Moody, Raymond A. (1977) *Reflections on Life After Life* **Mockingbird New York USA and** [paperback] **Bantam Books New York USA and also Corgi Books London ISBN 0-552-10814-6**

Moody, Raymond A. with Perry, Paul (1988) *The Light Beyond* **Macmillan London ISBN 0-333-45388-0 Also** [paperback] **Bantam Books New York USA ISBN 0-553-05285-3**

"The third of Raymond Moody's popular books on the NDE and his most considered treatment. Contains a number of intriguing cases that are hard to explain on the basis of purely physicalist theories … A good place to begin." (David Lorimer)

Sabom, Michael B. (1982) *Recollections of Death* Corgi Books London ISBN 0-552-12053-7

"One of the best scientific books on the subject. Sabom is a cardiologist who began with a sceptical view but came round to take the NDE and its consequences very seriously. A unique feature of the book is a comparison of six cases of apparently veridical out-of-body perception with a control group. The results showed that those claiming to have witnessed their resuscitation gave accurate pictures while those who simply imagined it made some major errors." (David Lorimer)

A more recent study by Sabom is:

Sabom, Michael B. (1998) *Light and Death. One doctor's fascinating account of near-death experiences* Zondervan Grand Rapids Michigan USA ISBN 0-310-21992-2

Following on from his first book, Sabom considers 47 new cases, all of whom have a Christian background, and his conclusions tend to be coloured by his own conservative Christian theology. However, the most important aspect of this book is the Pam Reynolds case, one of the most remarkable NDE accounts on record. The patient here was medically carefully monitored during a difficult brain operation, when the blood was drained, the heart was stopped and the body temperature was lowered. Following the operation the patient reported many out-of-the-body details of what was taking place during the operation which were confirmed by the medical staff.

Another of the pioneer workers in this field is **Dr Kenneth Ring**, Professor of Psychology at the University of Connecticut, whose publications have been at the heart of the literature on NDEs. His books are:

Ring, Kenneth (1980) *Life at Death. A scientific exploration of the near-death experience* William Morrow Co., New York USA ISBN 0-698110-32-3

Ring, Kenneth (1984) *Heading Toward Omega. In search of the meaning of the near-death experience* William Morrow Co. New York ISBN 0-688039-10-3

Ring, Kenneth (1992) *The Omega Project. Near-death experience, UFO encounters, and mind at large* William Morrow Co. New York ISBN 0-688107-29-X

Ring, Kenneth and Valarino, Evelyn E. (1998) *Lessons from the Light. What we can learn from the Near-Death Experience* Insight Books New York ISBN 0-306-45983-3

"A book that sums up Kenneth Ring's twenty years of NDE research by outlining the main conclusions to be drawn about the nature and significance of the NDE. Ring wrote one of the earliest scientific studies in *Life at Death* (1980) and followed this up with a study of the after-effects of NDEs in *Heading Towards Omega*. Here he collaborates with Evelyn Valarino, whose own earlier book *On the Other Side of Life* (1997) gives a good account of French thinking on the subject. A remarkable study but one to be read after other introductory books." (David Lorimer)

Dr Melvin Morse, a paediatrician, was the first to undertake extensive research into children's NDEs. This subject is the main topic of his first book:

Morse, Melvin L. with Perry, Paul (1990) *Closer to the Light. Learning from children's near-death experiences* **Villard Books New York USA First British edition (1991) Souvenir Press London ISBN 0-285-63030-X**

This study of NDEs in children is of particular value since it largely consists of the testimony of those too young to have absorbed cultural attitudes to death. There is also an appendix which reviews the scientific research on various drugs and other phenomena which have been used to explain NDEs from a conventional point of view. Morse uses this material to demonstrate that NDEs cannot be the result of hallucinations, etc., arising from the impact of various drugs, psychological phenomena or physiological stress.

In his second book he describes the results of the largest study of NDEs undertaken up to that time, in which he spreads his subject group to people of all ages:

Morse, Melvin L. with Perry, Paul (1992) *Transformed by the Light. The powerful effect of near-death experiences on people's lives* **Villard Books New York USA ISBN 0-679-40443-0 Reprinted (1993) BCA London CN2840 [no ISBN]**

"Dr Melvin Morse has made his name in writing about children's NDEs. Here he builds up a 'soul-based' hypothesis of the NDE while at the same time exploring the 'circuit boards of mysticism' in the right temporal lobe. His cases make a good argument for an encounter with the light as the key transformative element in the NDE, and which can be related more generally to mystical experiences." (David Lorimer)

Lorimer, David (1990) *Whole in One. The near-death experience and the ethic of interconnectedness* Arkana London ISBN 0-14-019258-1

"A book that takes a broader view of the NDE, setting it within a context of the history of religion, philosophy and more particularly ethics. Looks in detail at the life review and its ethical implications, arguing that the Golden Rule can be understood metaphysically as a natural consequence of an underlying unity of consciousness – from which an ethic of interconnectedness can be derived. A demanding read for those who would like to examine the spiritual and ethical implications of the NDE in more depth." (David Lorimer)

❧

Eadie, Betty J. (1995) *Embraced by the Light. What happens when you die* Thorsons London ISBN 1-85538-439-6 First published (1992) Gold Leaf Press Placerville CA USA

This is a remarkable book in that it has been described by Raymond Moody as "The most profound and complete near-death experience ever". Betty Eadie died after an operation in hospital and, over the next few hours, she had a most extensive and detailed NDE. During this time she experienced not only the classic stages of an NDE but also was exposed to a wide range of knowledge and understanding about 'life, the universe and everything'. As Melvin Morse states in the Foreword, "This book is really a textbook of the near-death experience, written as a simple and wonderful story that we can all understand."

❧

Brinkley, Dannion with Perry, Paul (1994) *Saved by the Light* Piatkus London ISBN 0-7499-1404-1 First published (1994) Villard Books New York USA

"The first of two books by Dannion Brinkley that give a graphic description of his shattering NDE resulting from a lightning strike. Brinkley's life review turned him round in a major way and makes dramatic reading. Very readable and gives a good sense of the personal implications of an NDE." (David Lorimer) Dr Raymond Moody, who wrote an introduction to the book, has called it: "The most amazing and complete near-death experience of the twenty thousand I have encountered" and Dr Melvin Morse has described it as "...the most detailed – and extraordinary – account of a near-death experience that I have ever read."

Brinkley, Dannion with Paul Perry (1995) *At Peace in the Light* HarperCollins New York USA Republished (1996) HarperPaperbacks New York USA ISBN 0-06-109446-3

The sequel to *Saved by the Light*, in which Brinkley describes how his extraordinary sense of perception and awareness of a wider reality resulting from his two near-death experiences has enabled him to help and inspire many, particularly those close to death.

Atwater, P.M.H. (1995) *Beyond the Light. Near-death experiences – the full story* **Thorsons London ISBN 1-85538-510-4** First published (1994) Carol Publishing Group New York NY USA ISBN 1-559-72229-0

Probably unique in the literature of this subject in that the author underwent three NDEs in the space of three months in 1977. These experiences led her to devote much of her time and energy thereafter to studying all aspects of the phenomenon and thus her book is a balance of both experience and research. Melvin Morse's Foreword states that the book "...provides a comprehensive overview of near-death research, skilfully combining science, religion, metaphysics, and her own research, synthesising the entire field."

Fenwick, Peter and Fenwick, Elisabeth (1995) *The Truth in the Light. An investigation of over 300 near-death experiences* **Headline London ISBN 0-7472-1186-8**

"The biggest UK study, using cases collected by the International Association of Near-Death Studies (UK). Provides an excellent and accessible overview of the field concluding that NDEs cannot be explained purely as brain events but point beyond. Introduces the idea of the 'paradox of unconsciousness' where the subject looks unconscious or dead from the outside but continues to experience a stream of self-consciousness." (David Lorimer)

Bailey, Lee W. & Yates, Jenny (1996) *The Near-Death Experience: A Reader* Routledge London ISBN 0-415-91431-0

For many enquirers seeking a wide-ranging introduction to the subject of NDEs this is a very good starting point. The book is made up of 24 contributions from many of the leading figures in the field of NDE research and experience, and each contribution is prefaced by a short introduction from the editors. Almost all the contributions are fascinating and very readable – only one or two may be difficult for the non-scientist. Overall it is an up-to-date and comprehensive survey of near-death studies and makes an excellent introduction to the subject.

Most NDEs are very positive, loving and transcendent experiences, but a relatively small proportion are negative, distressing, even horrific in their impact. The following book describes in detail one such negative experience which was, at least during the first part, almost unbelievably horrific:

Storm, Howard (2000) *My Descent Into Death. And the message of love which brought me back* Clairview London ISBN 1-902636-16-3

Howard Storm was an American academic who suffered a ruptured duodenal ulcer whilst on a trip to Paris. After hours of excruciating pain he 'died' and found himself in an out-of-the-body experience in which he was drawn into "fearsome realms of darkness and death, where he experienced the terrible consequences of a life of selfishness and materialism". Escaping from this situation, he was transported into regions of light where he experienced a more typical, positive NDE, during which he conversed with spiritual beings and gained a great deal of information about the meaning of life and death. His life was completely transformed by his experience and he was eventually ordained as a pastor in an American church.

(c) Research into Past-life Regression

The technique of Past-Life Regression runs very much in parallel with research into reincarnation in that both subjects are involved with the study of the previous lives of the individuals who are being investigated. However, past-life regression is not just concerned with the immediate past-life of, usually, a child who seems to remember events, places and individuals from this most recent incarnation. It usually involves adults who, under hypnosis, are taken back through their childhood, through the processes of birth and gestation, until they are able to recount details of one or more of their previous lives.

There are many books which describe either single cases of regression or recount some or many individual cases of this technique. Probably the best and most reliable of these books are those written by professionals, such as hypnotherapists or psychologists, who have sought to investigate the material on a scientific basis. The best cases are those where detailed material produced during a therapeutic session has been validated by subsequent historical research. In these cases the confirmatory material unearthed is often such as could not have been known to the individual under investigation. The following are some of the books available on this subject:

Grant, Joan and Kelsey, Denys (1970) *Many Lifetimes* **Victor Gollancz London ISBN 0-575-00173-9** First published (1969)

The material reported in this book is one of the pioneering studies which developed into modern past-life regression therapy. Joan Grant was a sensitive with highly developed extra-sensory faculties, in particular the faculty of "far memory" – the ability to recall details of her past lives. Becoming aware of it in the 1930s she used this ability to recall material which she developed into seven 'autobiographical novels' based on some of her earlier lives. Denys Kelsey was a psychiatrist who used hypnosis to regress patients to early periods of their lives.

Working together, eventually as a husband and wife team, they found that this process could be used to regress patients to relevant episodes in past lives, often with remarkable therapeutic results.

Iverson, Jeffrey (1976) *More Lives Than One? The evidence of the remarkable Bloxham Tapes* **Souvenir Press London ISBN 0-285-62239-0**

"Under hypnosis with Arnall Bloxham, one of the most respected hypnotherapists in Britain, [Jane Evans] a Welsh housewife describes in minute detail six quite separate lives: as a wife of a tutor in Roman times; as a Jew during the twelfth century massacre of Jews in York; as a serving girl to a French medieval merchant prince; as a maid of honour to Catherine of Aragon; as a poor serving girl in the London of Queen Ann; and finally as a nun in America."

The book largely consists of the detailed stories of these six past lives which form only one case among a unique collection of tape recordings made by Arnall Bloxham of regressions by four hundred men and women under hypnosis over a period of 20 years. Jeffrey Iverson, a television producer, researched the detail of these lives, finding much to indicate that the details of Jane Evans' lives were founded on fact. At the end of the book he states:

"So Bloxham's twenty years of work must constitute at least a *prima facie* case for reincarnation." He also produced a BBC documentary film, called "The Bloxham Tapes" based on all this material.

Underwood, Peter and Wilder, Leonard (1975) *Lives to Remember. A case book on reincarnation* **Robert Hall London ISBN 0-7091-5224-8**

The authors of this book are respectively an author and experienced psychical researcher, and a dentist and trained hypnotist. Their combined expertise was used to regress under hypnosis an ordinary housewife [Peggy Bailey] and then to assess, carefully, the results obtained and tape recorded verbatim. Under hypnosis Peggy Bailey relived three past lives: as 'Sally Fraser' in eighteenth century Devon; as 'Liza Bloggs' in the nineteenth century; and as 'Lady Alice Browning' in the early twentieth century. All the material obtained was carefully considered and discussed in relation to potential explanations other than reincarnation, such as self-delusion, hypnotic influence, psychic memories and multiple role-taking.

Wambach, Helen (1979) *Reliving Past Lives. The evidence under hypnosis* **Hutchinson London ISBN 0-09-136870-7**

Helen Wambach, a psychologist, developed a hypnotic technique by which she was able to regress her subjects back to previous lives. Over a period of 12 years, in a carefully designed project, she regressed more than 1000 subjects. Choosing specific time periods within an overall span of 4000 years she asked her subjects questions about their appearance, sex, clothing, lifestyle and feelings at the moment of death for each specific incarnation. Each subject was given a post-hypnotic suggestion that enabled them to fill out a data sheet following the session with precise details for each incarnation.

When analysed and correlated these data sheets provided "...striking and extraordinary evidence of the existence of reincarnation." Numerous figures, tables and specimen data sheets included in the text provide much useful information about conditions of life throughout the overall period – information which it was possible to confirm in many instances.

Dr Wambach also wrote a second book, *Life Before Life*, in which she describes a systematic exploration of the time before conception and birth. Using a group of 750 subjects she designed experiments in which large groups of people were hypnotically regressed and then prompted to visualise what had occurred to them in the interlife period immediately prior to their present life and during the processes of conception, growth of the foetus and birth. Following this process she then asked each subject immediately to fill in a questionnaire containing such questions about their prebirth memories as 'Did you choose to be born? How did you feel about beginning another life? Did you know your present mother before? What happened after conception?' The data from all the regressions were then compiled and analysed. Her book is a digest of the responses to a wide range of questions about the end of the interlife period and the processes of initiating another lifetime in a physical body.

Wambach, Helen (1979) *Life Before Life* **Bantam Books New York ISBN 0-553-12450-1**

Grof, Stanislav (1979) *Realms of the Human Unconscious. Observations from LSD research* **Souvenir Press London ISBN 0-285-64881-0** First published (1975) The Viking Press New York USA ISBN 0-670-59051-7

Stanislav Grof, a psychiatrist, spent many years investigating the use of the psychedelic drug LSD as a psychotherapeutic tool and in the wider investigation of the human unconscious. This book describes the results of his work and the development of a theory of the human psyche which is based on it. Chapter 5 is particularly useful in the context of this bibliography as it covers the wide range of transpersonal experiences elicited by the medical use of LSD. Among those he describes are past-life experiences, the awareness of events and experiences from individuals' past incarnations, ancestral experiences, descriptions of the way of life of the subject's biological ancestors – those of the same racial and cultural history as himself – and collective and racial experiences, an awareness often in detail of the cultures of other races or countries, frequently from the distant past. This material, although not necessarily direct evidence for human survival, comes from a different research field and nevertheless provides support and corroboration for much of the work on past-life regression.

Woolger, Roger J. (1987) Other *Lives, Other Selves. A Jungian psychotherapist discovers past lives* **Dolphin/Doubleday New York USA ISBN 1-85274-084-1 Also published (1990) Crucible/Aquarian Press Wellingborough Northants UK**

"One of the best books on hypnotic regression and its implications for psychotherapy. The author, originally a sceptic, is trained in Jungian analysis. Here he expands Jungian theory beyond childhood events and offers a holistic approach to altering destructive emotional patterns. With the help of case histories, he explores the connection between past life illness and current life fitness – both emotional and physical. He documents a number of psychological conditions that have responded to this approach." (Elisabeth Fenwick) A definitive work in this field.

TenDam, Hans (1990) *Exploring Reincarnation* **Arkana** (Penguin Books) **ISBN 0-14-019204-2 Republished (2003) Rider London ISBN 0-7126-6020-8** Originally published [Dutch] (1987)

"An excellent book for the serious student. Comprehensive and dispassionate, it begins with a consideration of the hypothesis and its history, moving on to experiences, including spontaneous recall, prebirth memories, regression and experiences around death. The third section is an extensive philosophical discussion of various possible views of the topic." (Elisabeth Fenwick)

Dr Brian Weiss is a psychiatrist who uses hypnosis as an important tool in the practice of psychotherapy. Originally his approach was that of a mainstream, orthodox practitioner who was entirely sceptical about anything as unscientific as parapsychology. However, following some remarkable experiences with a young patient called Catherine (recounted in his first book) he discovered and developed the healing potential of past-life therapy. During many years of clinical involvement in this field he has written three books in which he describes his experiences, including many case histories and explanatory commentaries. Overall his work provides much evidence supporting the concept of reincarnation, and thus survival. The books are:

Weiss, Brian L. (1994) *Many Lives, Many Masters. The true story of a prominent psychiatrist, his young patient and the past-life therapy that changed both their lives* **Piatkus Books London ISBN 0-7499-1378-9** Reprinted several times, most recently (2001) Previously published (1988) Simon & Schuster Inc. USA

Weiss, Brian L. (1995) *Through Time Into Healing. How past life regression therapy can heal mind, body and soul* **Judy Piatkus (Publishers) Ltd. London ISBN 0-7499-1477-7** First published (1992) Simon & Schuster Inc. New York USA ISBN 0-671-74528-X

Weiss, Brian L. (1996) *Only Love is Real. The story of soulmates reunited* **Judy Piatkus (Publishers) London ISBN 0-7499-1635-4** Previously published (1996) Warner Books Inc. New York USA ISBN 0-446-51945-6

Judy Hall is a counsellor and healer who has been running past-life exploration groups for more than twenty years. Among the books that she has written on this subject are:

Hall, Judy (1996) *Principles of Past Life Therapy* **Thorsons London ISBN 0-7225-3353-5**

Hall, Judy (1997) *Hands Across Time* **Findhorn Press Forres Moray Scotland ISBN 1-899171-61-4**

Hall, Judy (1998) *Deja Who? A new look at past lives* **Findhorn Press Forres Moray Scotland ISBN 1-899171-52-5**

Deja Who? is described as the first book that accepts reincarnation and yet questions the validity of some recalled past lives. Many famous names appear time after time in past-life regressions, and the most useful part of this book is where Judy Hall explores in depth the possible alternative explanations to reincarnation which may explain such occurrences. These may be suggestion, paramnesia, cryptomnesia, false memory syndrome, possession, psychiatric illness, multiple personality disorder, and others. The validity and relevance of past lives are examined in the context of these alternative explanations.

Newton, Michael (1996) *Journey of Souls* **Llewellyn Publications St Paul Minnesota USA ISBN 1-56718-485-5** First edition (1994)

Many books have described processes of hypnotic regression where people recall accounts of their past lives. This is described as the first book where, through hypnosis, individuals are helped to recall otherwise lost memories of the periods *between* former reincarnations on earth – in other words it provides accounts from 29 individual cases of details of the after-life. *Journey of Souls* not only provides detailed accounts of the processes of death and progression through the after-life; more importantly, using a new technique, it confirms information originally determined by traditional methods using mediums.

The description of this book as being the first to recall memories of the periods between incarnations is not strictly correct. Others have published accounts of how, using similar techniques, they have also brought to light details of their clients' experiences between lives lived on earth. A very good example of such accounts is:

Whitton, Joel L. and Fisher, Joe (1986) *Life Between Life. Scientific explorations into the void separating one incarnation from the next* **Grafton Books London ISBN 0-246-13024-5**

Dr Whitton is a Canadian psychiatrist who uses hypnosis to take his patients back into their former lives and also to seek details of the periods in between such lives in what he calls the *bardo* state. Joe Fisher is a British author and journalist who has written previously on the theme of reincarnation (see p 32). The first part of their book, *Life Between Life,* is a wide-ranging discussion of reincarnation, descriptions of the interlife periods 'out-of-the-body' – based on information Dr Whitton has obtained from patients – and a consideration of the implications of such information for life and living. The second half, *Karmic Case Studies*, is a selection of six cases which graphically illustrate both the techniques and the results obtained from them. A valuable addition to the literature on survival and reincarnation.

Bowman, Carol (1997) *Children's Past Lives. How past life experiences can affect your child* **Element Books Shaftesbury Dorset UK ISBN 1-86204-149-0 First published (1997) Bantam Books New York USA**

Carol Bowman describes how, almost by chance, she discovered that her two children's phobias were the result of past-life traumas and how, through hypnosis, these problems could be brought to the surface, recognised and cleared. Following this up with training in past-life therapy, an extensive study of the literature and many interviews with other parents, she has brought together a great deal of useful new information about the past-life experiences of children.

Children's Past Lives is divided into three sections. The first consists of her own family's story, together with many other cases of children's past-life memories. There are also summaries of the work of other researchers in this field, such as Helen Wambach, Edith Fiore and Roger Woolger. She devotes an entire chapter (Ch 6) to the work of Professor Ian Stevenson, providing a valuable introduction to this seminal research which is not easily accessed by the ordinary reader. The second section provides guidance to parents in recognising and handling children's spontaneous past-life memories. The third section considers children's insights into the nature of life and death.

Bowman, Carol (2002) *Return From Heaven. Beloved relations reincarnated within your family* **Thorsons London ISBN 0-00-713231-X** First published (2001) HarperCollins London

In her second book, Carol Bowman develops her theme of the past-life experiences of children. She concentrates on many cases of families where departed relatives have apparently reincarnated back into the same family and her studies suggest that this phenomenon may be relatively common. Many of her cases are usefully discussed in the context of the research of other workers in this field.

Davies, Mary (1999) *The Journey. A spiritual autobiography spanning two thousand years* **Published privately by the author ISBN 0-9536398-0-0** Obtainable from Mary Davies Ardgowan House Shore Road Brodick Isle of Arran KA27 8AJ Scotland

"The author is a practising healer and past-life therapist who, in this book, has used six of her own past lives and her present life to weave a fascinating account of how the human soul evolves over the centuries, making mistakes and learning valuable lessons, and how the continuing process is a spiritual journey to the Cosmic Source of Divine Love. The style is conversational, deceptively easy to read but containing deep wisdom."

Cannon, Dolores (2003) *Between Death and Life. Conversations with a spirit* **Gateway Books Dublin Eire ISBN 0-7171-3622-1** First published (1993) Ozark Mountain Publishers Huntsville AR USA

Dolores Cannon is an experienced past-life regression therapist who has brought together many years of research into the inter-life period between death and a further incarnation. Based mainly on the question and answer sessions between herself and individual subjects, she provides an introduction to the range of experiences that souls are faced with after death, the different conditions and levels of existence that are found in the spirit realms and how and why individuals return to earth for a subsequent incarnation.

As a wayfarer takes a brief lodging,
so he that is travelling through the way of existence
finds in each birth but a passing rest.

Bodhicharyavatara (Buddhism)

৯

Like a grain a mortal ripens.
Like a grain he is born hither again.

Katha Upanishad, i, 6 (Hindu)

৯

Naked didst thou come,
naked shalt thou go;
Thou shalt become a morsel for death,
and return to a body again and again.

Arjan, iii, 152 (Sikhism)

4 Seers and Mystics
Personal Experiences and Writings

Throughout human history there have always been prophets, seers and visionaries who, in a variety of ways, have apparently been able to 'see' beyond present time and space. Not only have they been able to see into the past and the future, they have also been able to visualise, often in detail, the realities of the spiritual world which is all about us but remains unseen by most people. Their descriptions of the spirit world and the spiritual philosophy which often accompanies them clearly demonstrate that, for these individuals at least, the reality of our survival of death and the continuity of life on 'the other side' is certain. There are many such seers whose writings could be used to support survival. However four well known figures who lived in the West during the past 350 years are quoted as good examples of this type of evidence.

(a) Emanuel Swedenborg

Emanuel Swedenborg was born in 1688 into a wealthy Swedish family in Stockholm and initially received a classical education at the University of Uppsala. However, he showed a great interest in science and technology and went on to study all of the mathematical and physical sciences that were then available. He travelled extensively throughout Europe and spent several periods of his life in London, where he died in 1772. During his adult life he showed himself to be a brilliant scientist and scholar and had a particular aptitude for the invention of mechanical devices. His scientific and inventive abilities attracted the attention of the King of Sweden who appointed him to be Assessor Extraordinary of the Royal Board of Mines.

Between 1716 and 1734 Swedenborg wrote extensively about the physical sciences and, particularly, on metallurgical subjects. From 1734 to 1742 he turned his attention to the study of human anatomy and physiology and published widely in these subject areas. In both of these fields he suggested many ideas and theories which have only become accepted and developed further by science during the last century. For example, Swedenborg was the first to indicate that the cortical areas of the brain are the specific seat of the higher faculties of the mind. In spite of all this work his aim was not primarily to further scientific research as such, but to find the seat of the human soul in the body and to demonstrate its existence. In 1743 a remarkable event took place in Swedenborg's life which caused him to change his whole approach to his work. He apparently underwent a series of dreams and mystical experiences which he described in a later letter as "I have been called to a holy office by the Lord Himself, who most graciously manifested Himself in person to me, His servant, in the year 1743; when He opened my sight to the view of the spiritual world, and granted me the privilege of conversing with spirits and angels, which I enjoy to this day". He also wrote, in 1745, of having been admitted into the kingdom of God 'by the Messiah Himself' and speaking there with various heavenly personages and 'with the dead who have risen again'. After this he gave up all his previous work, recognising that these studies had only been the preparation for a much more important mission to which he had to devote the rest of his life.

Over the next 29 years he undertook a profound study of the Bible and wrote prolifically on the themes which developed from this study. His major work *Arcana Caelestia* (or Heavenly Secrets – he wrote in Latin) was published in eight large volumes between 1749 and 1756 and was principally a revelation of the inner or spiritual meaning of the Books of Genesis and Exodus. Subsequently he published further major volumes and many minor books developing themes from the *Arcana* and unfolding on a wider scale the inner spiritual meaning of the Bible. This enormous output of esoteric scholarship was founded on his continuing direct contact with beings, or angels as he called them, in the spiritual world. As he stated not long before his death – "It has pleased the Lord to … open the interiors of my mind or spirit, whereby I have been permitted to be in the spiritual world with angels, and at the same time in the natural world with people, and this now [has happened for] twenty-seven years."

Swedenborg's writings are very concentrated and, particularly in the older translations, may be found to be heavy going by many wishing to explore his spiritual philosophy. The following books are suggested as a way into the subject for those wishing to know more about his teachings on life after death and related subjects:

Stanley, Michael (1988) *Emanuel Swedenborg: Essential Readings* **Crucible New York USA ISBN 1-85274-026-4**

Following an introduction on the life and work of Swedenborg and an outline of the structure of his spiritual thought, Michael Stanley has selected and edited many readings covering the whole range of his visionary insights. This book is a useful general introduction to the subject.

Fox, Leonard and Rose, Donald L. (editors) (1996) *Conversations with Angels. What Swedenborg heard in heaven* **Chrysalis Books West Chester Pennsylvania USA ISBN 0-87785-177-8**

"Throughout the final twenty-seven years of his life, Swedenborg explored the realms of heaven and hell and spoke with angels about the nature of life after death, discussed with newly arrived spirits their misconceptions about the afterlife, and debated with devils or spirits from hell. As an Enlightenment scholar, Swedenborg recorded these encounters, attesting to God's will that humanity might know the truth of eternal life. These narratives have been selected from three of Swedenborg's works, *Conjugial Love, Apocalypse Revealed,* and *The True Christian Religion,* and have been arranged by theme. Swedenborg's conversations with angels startle the reader with insights into the reality of the spiritual world."

Swedenborg, Emanuel (1989) *Heaven and its Wonders and Hell. From things seen and heard* **The Swedenborg Society London** No ISBN Translated from the original 1758 Latin (1958) Reprinted (1989)

This book, usually known as *Heaven and Hell*, is one of Swedenborg's original works. It has been described as follows: "First published in 1758, this remarkable work is a detailed description of life after death, reported by Swedenborg from his actual visionary journeys to heaven and hell. Our entrance into the spiritual world, the nature of the world of spirits, and the place of preparation for our eternal dwelling place are explained. The structure and life of heaven and hell, uses of angelic societies, the marriage of angelic spirits, children in heaven, angelic language, and many other topics are discussed in this famous work."

A useful introductory summary of Swedenborg's life and works was written some years ago by William Le Geyt (*Swedenborg's Radical Christianity,* The Friends' Quarterly Vol 19, No 1, January 1975 pp 39-43) In it he gives an outline of Swedenborg's description of the after-life, as follows "Thirdly, he gives a credible account of life after death, which is in general accord with what evidence there is from psychical research. He claims to have been granted the privilege of prolonged access to the spiritual world for the purposes of his mission. Basically, he describes the future life as a full and active one where there is an appearance of a physical world, but where time, space and visible objects have a quite different nature from their counterparts in this world. Individuals retain their more basic attitudes and abilities, and gravitate towards different communities on the principle of 'like to like'. There are of course evil communities, but divine intervention, far from being punitive, is concerned only to ameliorate their conditions."

(b) William Blake

William Blake (1757-1827) was a poet, painter, engraver, prophet and visionary who lived at a time when religion was at a low ebb in England and when the materialist philosophy which developed from the work of Bacon, Newton and Locke was taking an increasingly strong hold, particularly in science. Blake was born in London and lived almost the whole of his life there. He was the second son of a lower middle class hosier who never sent his son to school; instead, he helped him to develop his obvious early talents as an artist. At the age of fourteen he was apprenticed to an engraver and it was through the exercise of this craft that he earned a somewhat precarious livelihood throughout his adult years. His skill and genius as an artist, a poet and a spiritual visionary went almost unrecognised during his lifetime. This was probably because his spiritual approach to life was considered to be out of date or even beyond the comprehension of many of his contemporaries, and he was able to sell very little of his own artistic output.

From a very early age he had visions and was aware of the reality of the spiritual world. At the age of four he saw God looking in through the window and five years later he saw "a tree filled with angels, bright angelic wings bespangling every bough like stars". Such mystical visions and awareness remained with him for the rest of his life For example, in his mid-40s he lived for three years in a little cottage at Felpham on the Sussex coast and here, as Kathleen Raine tells us, he "saw angels descending on a ladder from heaven to his cottage, and the visions that came to him by the sea were among the most radiantly beautiful that he ever had." It was here that he also often saw fairies and once observed what he called a fairy's funeral.

Blake's over-arching vision of spiritual reality was such that it not only guided him throughout his life; it also drove him to undertake courses of action which would have seemed almost irrational to any ordinary person. What he called his 'Inspirers' would not let him escape from them, as: "I am under the direction of Messengers from Heaven, Daily & Nightly…" Most people would have adapted their output to the fashions of the day and earned a good income from sales of their work. Under the influence of his awareness of spiritual reality Blake was unable to do this and accordingly lived all his adult life on the edge of poverty. He concentrated instead in his writings and artistic output on taking issue with the materialist philosophy which sought, then as now, to separate humanity from an awareness of the spiritual reality behind the created universe. Interestingly from the point of view of this review, Blake claimed that a great deal of his work was produced under direct guidance – that it was essentially automatic writing arising from a source other than his normal consciousness, presumably in a similar way to the individuals recorded in Section 5 below. Thus in describing his book *Milton*, he states:

> "I have written this poem from immediate dictation, twelve or sometimes twenty lines at a time, without premeditation and even against my will. The time it has taken in writing was thus rendered nonexistent, and an immense poem exists which seems to be the labour of a long life, all produced without labour or study."

Blake does not say a great deal specifically about life after death as such, although it is clearly a part of his overall philosophy. However, there are some quotations from his writings where the concept of survival is understood or more directly indicated. The following instances are quoted by Kathleen Raine:

> 1 Blake strongly opposed the idea that humanity is constrained completely by space and time. There are two conditions for human life, confinement within a material body and the unconfined freedom of unimpeded energy when the 'spiritual body or angel' is released by death from the material body.

> 2 He often saw and communicated with human spirits from another plane of existence. His much loved younger brother Robert died at the early age of 20. Blake was present at his death and records that he saw his brother's spirit rising up through the ceiling 'clapping his hands for joy'. Blake later wrote in a letter:

>> "Thirteen years ago I lost a brother & with his spirit I converse daily and hourly in the Spirit & see him in my remembrance in the regions of my imagination. I hear his advice & even now write from his dictate."

>> Blake believed that it was his brother's spirit which gave him the secret of the process by which he produced the beautifully illuminated pages of his poems.

> 3 He drew pictures of the heads of some of his spiritual visitants. One of these is entitled *"The Man who taught Blake Painting"*.

Dr Don Morse (see p 91) has summarised Blake's concept of the after-life as follows, "Once you die, you leave the physical plane and your soul resides in the etheric plane for a few days. Your soul then travels to the astral plane, where it would attend spiritual classes and also enjoy the pursuit of music, art and other intellectual interests. On the astral plane you are not changed except for the lack of a physical body. After having progressed through the astral plane, your soul enters the mental planes. These are also eventually transcended, and your soul turns within to the real self. In doing so your soul casts off, one by one, all astral and mental layers. Your soul then goes on to higher and more subtle planes [travelling towards its eventual union with God]".

Kathleen Raine sums up Blake in the following words:

> "Take him as one will, as artist, poet, or religious revolutionary, Blake is a figure whose stature overtops all but the greatest men of genius that England has produced."

Caroline Spurgeon puts it more specifically when she says:

> "William Blake is one of the great mystics of the world; and he is by far the greatest and most profound who has spoken in English. Like Henry More and Wordsworth, he lived in a world of glory, of spirit and of vision, which, for him, was the only real world. At the age of four he saw God looking in at the window, and from that time until he welcomed the approach of death by singing songs of joy which made the rafters ring, he lived in an atmosphere of divine illumination."

There is an enormous literature covering the life and artistic output of William Blake but perhaps two fairly small books provide a rounded introduction to this subject. They are:

Raine, Kathleen (1951) *William Blake* **Longmans Green & Co. Harlow Revised version published (1965)**

Raine, Kathleen (1970) *William Blake* **Thames & Hudson London ISBN 0-500-20107-2**

Another small book, from which some of the above quotations were taken, and which gives a brief but powerful introduction to Blake, is:

Spurgeon, Caroline F. E. (1913) *Mysticism in English Literature* **pp 129-147 Cambridge University Press London**

❧

(c) Rudolf Steiner

Dr Rudolf Steiner (1861-1925) was, like Emanuel Swedenborg, both a scientist and a visionary. He was born in Austria, the eldest son of a village stationmaster in the country south of Vienna. Unlike Swedenborg, he was endowed from an early age with the faculties which enabled him to explore the spiritual world – but he did not admit openly to these abilities until he was about 40. Steiner was educated initially in a school specialising in science and mathematics but at the same time he taught himself the classics. By the time he came to leave school and go on to the Technical University in Vienna he had become convinced of the absolute reality of the world of spirit – the world that lay behind and beyond the experience of the physical senses. He knew, by direct experience, that the conclusions about the reality of the world which were propounded by scientific materialism were incorrect. At the university he studied the natural sciences with the intention of becoming a schoolmaster but he also became interested in the thoughts and writings of Goethe, eventually undertaking a thorough study of Goethe's scientific works.

After university Steiner began to earn his living as a private tutor and, remarkably for someone aged 23, in 1884 he was invited to edit and write an introduction to Goethe's scientific writings for an edition of the German Classics. In 1888 he was given an invitation which recognised the quality of his scholarship. He was asked to edit a new edition of Goethe's scientific works based on the original manuscript collection in the Goethe Archives at Weimar. By 1900 Steiner had established himself in the world and was coming up to 40 years of age, and from then on he dedicated himself to lecturing and writing about the spiritual – the 'supersensible' – world of which his increasingly developing spiritual faculties made him more and more aware. At first he became involved with Theosophy but eventually went on to develop his own system of spiritual thought. He called it Anthroposophy – the knowledge of the true being of man and of his relation to the universe; or, as Steiner himself defined the term, "the consciousness of one's humanity". The Anthroposophical Society was founded in 1913. Thereafter Rudolf Steiner dedicated himself to writing books, lecturing and conducting specialist courses on the many themes arising from his knowledge of spiritual reality, seeking to lead mankind into a new spiritual understanding of humanity and the universe. His intention in all these activities was to initiate a universal 'science of the spirit'.

Over the years Steiner's output of work was enormous, covering not only the interrelationships between the physical and spiritual worlds, but also developing new ideas and methods in the fields of education, agriculture, art and medicine. Rather like Swedenborg, his books do not always make easy reading for the uninitiated. A very readable and comprehensive introduction to his life and works is:

Shepherd, A. P. (1975) *A Scientist of the Invisible. An introduction to the life and work of Rudolf Steiner* **Hodder & Stoughton London ISBN 0-340-01752-X** First published (1954)

≈

A more recent series of three small books by Roy Wilkinson provides a valuable digest of Steiner's spiritual philosophy. They are:

Wilkinson, Roy (1993) *Rudolf Steiner. Aspects of his spiritual world-view. Anthroposophy volume 1* **Temple Lodge Publishing London ISBN 0-04693-47-3**

The four chapters are: Rudolf Steiner – herald of a new age.

Reincarnation and karma.

The spiritual nature of the human being.

The development of human consciousness.

Wilkinson, Roy (1993) *Rudolf Steiner. Aspects of his spiritual world-view. Anthroposophy volume 2* **Temple Lodge Publishing London ISBN 0-904693-51-1**

The four chapters are: Evolution of the world and humanity.

Relationships between the living and the dead.

Forces of evil.

The modern path of initiation.

Wilkinson, Roy (1994) *Rudolf Steiner. Aspects of his spiritual world-view. Anthroposophy volume 3* **Temple Lodge Publishing London ISBN 0-90463-63-5**

The four chapters are: Life between death and rebirth.

The spiritual hierarchies.

The philosophical approach to the spirit.

The mission of Christ.

At least one chapter in all three books covers a subject relating to survival, life after death or reincarnation.

≈

Steiner himself wrote more than 30 books and many essays, and also delivered over 6,000 lectures across Europe. All the latter were recorded. Most of this material has been published in English translation so that there is an enormous record of Steiner's research into spiritual reality available to the interested reader. The following three books provide an introduction to Steiner's views on survival and associated subject areas:

Steiner, Rudolf (1969) *Occult Science. An introduction* **Rudolf Steiner Press London ISBN 0-85440-208-X** New translation by G. & M. Adams of original 1909 edition

In this volume, Chapter III considers death and the processes of severance from the body, past-life review and entry into the spiritual world, conditions in the spirit world and approaching a new incarnation. Chapter VI, among other things, looks at the etheric body, the astral world and man's life after death.

Steiner, Rudolf (1999) *Founding a Science of the Spirit* **Rudolf Steiner Press London ISBN 1-85584-077-4**

In this group of 14 lectures, originally given in 1906, "...Steiner speaks with great clarity and precision on the fundamental nature of the human being in relation to the cosmos, the evolution of the earth, the journey of the soul after death, reincarnation and karma, good and evil, and the modern path of meditative training. Throughout, Steiner's emphasis is on a scientific exposition of spiritual phenomena."

Steiner, Rudolf (2000) *Rosicrucian Wisdom. An introduction* **Rudolf Steiner Press London ISBN 1-85584-063-4**

In a further group of 14 lectures, given in 1907, Steiner reinterprets Rosicrucian teaching describing, among other things, "...the law of destiny, the fact of life after death, ways of developing spiritual vision and humanity's past and future evolution."

Drake, Stanley (2002) *Though You Die. Death and life beyond death* **Floris Books Edinburgh Scotland ISBN 0-86315-369-0**

This is the "Fourth edition of a book first published in 1962 which relates Rudolf Steiner's understanding of death and beyond, but which also draws on other experiences and insights. The result is both informative and illuminating. In a short book the author conveys many essentials of a spiritual philosophy of life and death." (David Lorimer)

(d) Edgar Cayce

Edgar Cayce (1877-1945) had one of the most remarkable psychic gifts that have been recognised during the past 150 years. He was able to put himself into a hypnotic sleep and, when the names and locations of sick people were given to him, he could diagnose their conditions accurately and prescribe the means by which they could be cured. Often the treatments were simple, homely recipes or applications but they seemingly rarely failed to bring about an improvement of the conditions when they were given as prescribed. Cayce was born in Christian County in Kentucky of farming stock and right from early childhood he was endowed with 'second sight', the ability to be aware of the spiritual world and to access all sorts of information normally unavailable to ordinary folk. Thus he could 'sleep on' a publishers catalogue by putting it under his pillow at night and in the morning would know all the details of the books contained in it. He was also deeply religious, knowing the Bible well, and had the ambition to become a preacher or a doctor, but there was never enough money to undertake the training.

It seemed that he was destined to become a psychic healer because, every time as a young man he tried to forget his gifts and lead a normal life in a 'straight' job, strange things happened to prevent him from following his wishes. For example, at one time he got a good job as an insurance salesman but, within days, he had completely lost his voice and, for the rest of his life, he never entirely recovered the ability to speak fully and clearly.

Eventually, circumstances led him to discover the technique of entering a hypnotic sleep and, on prompting with the name of a patient, to diagnose their illness and prescribe a remedy for it. For forty years afterwards he regularly followed this routine for thousands of patients; no matter where the individuals were in the world, Cayce's gift enabled him to contact them subconsciously, diagnose their problems and offer a treatment. He also answered questions about the patients which provided further useful information about their conditions and general lifestyle. For many years the information requested from Cayce related specifically to physical illnesses but eventually he began to widen his scope. It appeared that the 'higher source' from which he obtained his information about individual's problems was almost unlimited. As he was prompted by wider and wider questioning he was able to speak with authority on an enormous range of subjects of a philosophical, spiritual and factual nature.

Right from the start careful notes were taken of all Cayce's "readings" and these were typed up and filed as a record of what had transpired. Over the 40 years of his work more than 30,000 readings were obtained and these were stored in an archive at the Association for Research and Enlightenment (ARE), at Virginia Beach, Virginia, which he founded. Since his death an enormous amount of work has been undertaken on these records by the ARE and many books have been produced distilling the wisdom and information that Edgar Cayce subconsciously produced over many years of fruitful work. The topics covered by these books include the paranormal world, reincarnation and past lives and dream interpretation.

Several biographies of Edgar Cayce have been written describing both his life story and the application and outcome of his extraordinary gifts. Among these are:

Millard, Joseph (1961) *Edgar Cayce. Man of miracles* **Neville Spearman London**

Sugrue, Thomas (1967) *There is a River: The story of Edgar Cayce* **Dell Publishing Co. New York USA ISBN 0-440-38680-2**

Stearn, Jess (1974) *The Sleeping Prophet: an examination of the work of Edgar Cayce* **Frederick Muller London ISBN 0-584-00266-1** Originally published (1967) Doubleday New York USA

Smith, Robert A. (1997) *The Lost Memoirs of Edgar Cayce. Life as a seer* **ARE Press Virginia Beach VA USA ISBN 0-876043-93-7**

Bro, Harmon H. (1989) *Edgar Cayce. A Seer out of Season* **Aquarian Press Wellingborough Northants UK ISBN 0-85030-937-9** Originally published (1989) New American Library New York USA

This is probably the definitive biography of Edgar Cayce. Dr Bro worked for a year with Cayce in 1944 and using the information he gained from this time, together with many hundreds of interviews with the family, friends and associates of Cayce, he produced an in-depth account of his life and work.

A number of books on specific subjects have been compiled from the Edgar Cayce records. Some of those which are pertinent to the subject of survival are:

Agee, Doris (1989) edited by Hugh Lynn Cayce *Edgar Cayce on ESP* Aquarian Press Wellingborough Northants UK

Langley, Noel (1989) edited by Hugh Lynn Cayce *Edgar Cayce on Reincarnation* Aquarian Press Wellingborough Northants UK Originally published (1967) Warner Books New York USA

Smith, Robert C. (1990) edited by Charles Thomas Cayce *Edgar Cayce on Remembering your Past Lives* Aquarian Press Wellingborough Northants UK Originally published (1989)

The literature on the life and work of Edgar Cayce is enormous; more than 200 books are listed in the US Library of Congress catalogue. The selection given above is only a small fraction of the available material.

5 Shamans and Shamanism

The previous section considered the evidence for survival presented by the cases of four well known seers who were born with, or were granted later in life, great visionary gifts which enabled them to describe the world of spirit. This section will briefly consider another type of seer, people who do not occur sporadically but who come from a long, continuous tradition which goes back in time to well before written records of human history became available – the shamans.

Shamanism can be considered to be the oldest spiritual path on earth with its origins going back perhaps 50,000 years. It is not a religion or a belief system but a way of seeking, exploring and using for human benefit direct knowledge of the spiritual world, which is the primary reality and the source of the material world in which we live. It has been said that the shaman is someone who walks with one foot in the everyday world and one foot in the spirit world. Shamanism has always been found among traditional, tribal, cultures, particularly in Siberia – where the name *shaman* comes from – North, Central and South America, Africa, South East Asia, Australia and the Pacific islands. Although these traditional cultures have shrunk considerably in the face of the pressures first from Christian missionaries and more recently from Western scientific materialism, shamanism still survives in its original form in most of its original centres. More remarkably, there has been a recent re-appearance of shamanism in Western countries, where such ideas might be assumed to have died out long ago.

A shaman is someone, woman or man, who normally having undergone a long training 'apprenticed' to an already established shaman, gains the ability to function effectively in both worlds. This is made possible by being able to enter into a state of altered consciousness, usually brought about by the use of techniques such as drumming or the ingestion of psychotropic plants. Such a state of altered consciousness can be likened to an out-of-the-body experience in that the individual leaves his or her body and 'travels' in the spiritual world seeking knowledge and the ability to help members of their community.

Two definitions provided by experts provide a useful summary of the role of the shaman:

> "A shaman is a man or woman who enters an altered state of consciousness – at will – to contact and utilize an ordinarily hidden reality in order to acquire knowledge, power, and to help other persons."
> (Harner, 1990 page 20)

"[Shamans are] tribally assigned magico-religious professionals who deliberately alter their consciousness on order to obtain information from the spirit world. They use this knowledge and power to help and to heal members of their tribe, as well as the tribe as a whole." Krippner, S. & Welch, P. (1992) *Spiritual Dimensions of Healing: From Native Shamanism to Contemporary Health Care* p 27. Irvington NY USA

It is not possible here to give any real idea of the breadth and depth of the significance of shamanism in relation not only to the concept of survival but also to the understanding of the spiritual world on a wider scale. The selection of books listed below provides a useful introduction to shamanism and a more extensive list of sources and bibliography is provided in Harner (1990), Drury (1989) and Rutherford (1996).

Eliade, Mircea (1964) *Shamanism. Archaic techniques of ecstasy* **Routledge & Kegan Paul London**. Originally published [French] (1951) Republished [paperback] Arkana (1989) ISBN 0-14-19155-0

Eliade's book is one of the classic works, possibly *the* classic work, on shamanism. However, the academic approach and style does not make it easy reading.

ॐ

Harner, Michael (1990) *The Way of the Shaman* **HarperCollins New York USA 3rd edition ISBN 0-06-250373-1** Originally published (1980) Harper & Row

Another classic work, written by an anthropologist who is also a trained and practising shaman.

ॐ

Drury, Neville (1989) *The Elements of Shamanism* **Element Books Shaftesbury Dorset UK ISBN 1-85230-069-8**

A useful introductory text.

ॐ

Rutherford, Leo (1996) *Thorsons Principles of Shamanism* **Thorsons London ISBN 0-7225-3321-7**

One of the best introductory books written by an engineer who 'gave it all up' to train and practice as a shaman.

ॐ

Rahesha, Namua (1994) *The Serpent and the Circle. A practical guide to shamanism* **Judy Piatkus London ISBN 0-7499-1388-6**

An essentially practical guide to shamanism, intended not only to introduce the subject to the uninitiated but also providing numerous exercises to enable the beginner to set out on a path of discovery of the non-ordinary reality of the spiritual world.

Two other authors are well known for their accounts of their involvement in South American shamanism. Both were scientifically trained before going on to study shamanistic techniques in depth. Both have written a series of books on their experiences and examples of each of these series are:

Castenada, Carlos (1990) *Tales of Power* **Arkana London ISBN 0-14-19237-9** First published (1974) USA

Villoldo, Alberto (2001) *Shaman, Healer, Sage. How to heal yourself and others with the energy medicine of the Americas* **Bantam Books London ISBN 0-553-81380-3** First published Crown Publishers/Random House USA

Villoldo's book deals mainly with the concepts and practices of shamanic healing; however the last chapter, *Death, Dying and Beyond,* deals with the shaman's approach to dying and life beyond death.

Being born from out the state of birth-and-death
that giveth birth to mortal life, I now, set free,
pass to the state transcending birth.

A Mithraic Ritual

৵

As a man casts off worn-out clothes,
and puts on other new clothes,
so the spirit casts off worn-out bodies,
and puts on other new bodies.

Krishna. Bhagavad-Gita, ii, 22

৵

Among them [the Druids] the doctrine of Pythagoras had force,
namely, that the souls of men are undying,
and that after a fixed number of years they begin to live again,
the soul passing into another body.

Diodorus of Sicily

6 The Experiences and Accounts of Mediums and Sensitives

Since the beginning of the modern period of interest in psychic matters and survival in the middle of the nineteenth century, there have been many gifted people – usually called mediums or sensitives – who have offered their services to help those seeking information about these subjects. Either to gain knowledge about, and communication with, those members of their families who have died; or to further the cause of psychic research so that human beings can gain a greater understanding about the purpose of life and their place in the universe. Many of these individuals have written autobiographical accounts of their activities or have had books written about their lives as sensitives.

Mediums are usually divided into two groups, 'mental' and 'physical' mediums. Mental mediums operate through extra sensory perception (ESP), a heightened degree of awareness of the spiritual world, in that they seek to communicate with discarnate spirits through clairvoyance (inner sight) or clairaudience (inner hearing). Another manifestation of mental mediumship is that of 'automatic writing', where communications from the other side are transmitted through the handwriting of the medium – normally in a script totally unlike that of the individual sensitive. Physical mediums are those who demonstrate psycho-kinetic (PK) phenomena: the ability to produce raps and similar noises, the levitation or movement of objects – often heavy furniture – moving lights, touches by seemingly 'ghostly' hands, and apports (the production of objects apparently out of nowhere). 'Direct voice' is a form of physical mediumship where the voices of spirit communicators are produced, not directly from the medium but from close by. Materialisation mediums are those who, by production of the substance ectoplasm, are able to build up semblances of the dead which – in the best examples – have appeared in a form identical to their original living counterparts – and often recognised as such by their bereaved relatives. Mediums may operate in full consciousness or in trance; in the latter state they are temporarily taken over by a spirit 'control' or 'guide', or by other entities introduced by the control.

The following section consists of a list of the books giving accounts of the work of a selection of the better known sensitives particularly of the mid and later twentieth century.

Geraldine Cummins was an author and playwright who was also a medium with a remarkable gift for automatic writing. Of the 22 books she wrote 15 were 'transmitted' or produced by automatic writing. Amongst many other writings, she produced a series of scripts purporting to come from F.W.H. Myers, one of the distinguished scholars who founded the Society for Psychical Research in 1882 and who, after his death in 1901, was the instigator of the "Cross Correspondences" which provided much evidence in favour of survival. The present material gives a wide-ranging description of the conditions after death and many other details, particularly how the soul may progress up through ever higher spiritual levels or 'planes'. Miss Cummins produced two sets of material from Myers, during the 1920s and in 1933-4, and these were published as two books:

Cummins, Geraldine (1932) *The Road to Immortality. Being a description of the after-life purporting to be communicated by the late F.W.H. Myers through Geraldine Cummins* Foreword by Sir Oliver Lodge. With evidence of the survival of human personality by E.B. Gibbes. **Ivor Nicholson & Watson London. Republished (1955) Aquarian Press London**

One particularly useful part of this book is the foreword in which Sir Oliver Lodge confirms, through an independent channel, that Myers' scripts were "…a serious attempt to give information about a future life and the stages through which earnest people may expect to pass."

Cummins, Geraldine (1935) *Beyond Human Personality. Being a detailed description of the future life purporting to be communicated by the late F.W.H. Myers. Containing an account of the gradual development of the human personality into cosmic personality* **Ivor Nicholson & Watson London**

Amongst other books Miss Cummins also wrote:

Cummins, Geraldine (1948) *Travellers in Eternity* **Psychic Press London**

Cummins, Geraldine (1951) *Unseen Adventures. An autobiography covering thirty-four years of work in psychical research* **Rider London**

And:

Cummins, Geraldine (1965) *Swan on a Black Sea. A study in automatic writing: The Cummins-Willett scripts* **Edited by Signe Toksvig. Routledge & Kegan Paul London**

Mrs. Willett is the pseudonym of Mrs. Winifred Coombe Tennant who, during her lifetime, had been a gifted medium and automatic writer. Together with several other sensitives, she had been the vehicle for communications of a most remarkable kind, the Cross Correspondences (see p 16), which apparently came from the surviving spirits of F.W.H. Myers, Edmund Gurney and other early members of the Society for Psychical Research. Mrs. Coombe Tennant died in August 1956 and about a year later she began to communicate through the automatic writing of Geraldine Cummins. Over a period of two and a half years a series of 40 scripts were produced containing material of considerable evidential importance.

The book consists of a very long (50 page) Foreword by Professor C. D. Broad which contains, among other things, a lengthy synopsis of the main contents of the scripts and a critical analysis of their content. Then follow the scripts themselves and two short descriptive pieces by Geraldine Cummins, 'Personal Background' and 'Lines of Communication'. The value of this book is summarised in the following review:

> "What is quite certain is that this is a very important book indeed, and one which should be obligatory reading for all of the many of us who cannot yet bring ourselves to believe that human beings experience anything at all after the death of their bodies. Whatsoever our preconceptions may be, these scripts provide something solid and incontrovertible which cannot be explained away with the usual facility of the naturally incredulous" (Philip Toynbee, in *The Observer*)

Anthony Borgia was a medium with a strong gift of clairaudience who became the channel for several books which were published around the middle of the last century. The source of the material in these books was a one-time Catholic priest, Monsignor Robert Hugh Benson, a son of Edward White Benson a former Archbishop of Canterbury. Borgia came to know Benson personally in 1909 about five years before the latter died. Before his death Benson was a well known preacher and writer but, following his passing over to the spirit world, he apparently came to realise that much of the Church's teaching as well as what he had preached and written were wrong. With the intention of attempting to put this right, and to produce an account of life in the spirit and its meaning and purpose – he eventually communicated his story by clairaudience through Borgia, who wrote it down verbatim. Initially the material in these books was written in a narrative style, as an account of his passing through death to the spirit world and his initial exploration of his new 'abode', in the company of another recently deceased person Ruth, under the guidance of Edwin, an old friend and priestly colleague. Later material was published in a less personal, but more descriptive style. Borgia states that in order to establish the authenticity of the scripts and to seek an independent verification of them, he undertook a series of sittings with a medium of known integrity. By this means he was able to contact Benson directly and to receive confirmation of what he, Borgia, had written. The books containing these scripts are:

Borgia, Anthony (1942) *Beyond This Life* **Feature Books Ltd. London**

Borgia, Anthony (1954) *Life in the World Unseen* **Odhams Press London** Reprinted [many times but most recently] *(2002)* as *Life in the World Unseen. Spirit scripts from Monsignor Robert Hugh Benson recorded by Anthony Borgia* **Two Worlds Publishing Co. London ISBN 0-947823-46-8**

Borgia, Anthony (1957) *More about Life in the World Unseen* **Citadel Press New York USA**

Borgia, Anthony (1959) *Here and Hereafter* **Odhams Press London**

Life in the World Unseen is essentially an extended version of *Beyond this Life.*

John Campbell Sloan was a well known direct-voice medium in Scotland during the first half of the twentieth century. Between 1942 and 1945 a group of people met in Glasgow together with Sloan for a series of séances and all the material produced was recorded verbatim by a skilled stenographer. Subsequently, Arthur Findlay edited and prepared for publication the shorthand records of 19 of these séances, during which many communications from the 'other side' had come through. This material was published as:

Findlay, Arthur (1968) *Where Two Worlds Meet. Conversations between this world and the next* **Psychic Press Ltd. London** Originally published (1951) Psychic Press

The book contains a large amount of evidence supporting the concept of survival; there is much detail on the spiritual world and the conditions of life of its inhabitants. However, because the material was recorded verbatim, there is no structured account of conditions in the spiritual world. The information is given in a rather piecemeal fashion.

Jane Sherwood was a Quaker who died, aged 96, in May 1990. She was drawn, somewhat unwillingly, into psychic investigations following the death of her husband in the First World War and discovered that she had the gift of automatic writing. Using this gift she produced several books which tell us a great deal about death and the afterlife.

Sherwood, Jane (1991) *The Country Beyond. The doctrine of rebirth* C.W. Daniel Saffron Walden Essex UK ISBN 0-85207-254-6 Originally published (1969) Neville Spearman Ltd.

The following review provides a summary of the book's content:

"Books which have strongly influenced one's life can be likened to old friends, rare and beloved, to which one can turn again and again for truth and wisdom. Such a book, to my mind, is Jane Sherwood's *The Country Beyond*. The author started her investigations when her husband was killed in the First World War. She could not accept either that Andrew was no more or that he might survive in a realm where there was no use for his own energy and enquiring intellect. A valuable section of the book describes what befell the author when she set out to try to contact her husband.

"She was not in touch with anyone who was qualified to advise or warn her, and throughout many years endured frustrating, misleading experiences and dangers of which she had innocently been unaware. If for no other reason the book should be valued for the advice given to all who pursue psychic investigations.

"Jane Sherwood came through it all having three supreme advantages: unshakable Christian faith, a keen logical mind and sound common sense. Finally, through unflagging determination, she found herself to have the gift of automatic writing. She achieved her ambition of contact with her husband, and also with two other communicators. Subject matter includes descriptions of the active, progressing life 'beyond', analysis of the human entity – ourselves – *i e* descriptions of the four bodies or modes we all have, reincarnation, and the esoteric order within our solar system. With characteristic humility the author describes her book as a 'starting point' for others to work from." (Jean Snow, in *The Quarterly Review of the Churches' Fellowship*)

Of particular value spiritually are the later chapters, especially the last two, which deal in esoteric terms with the development of the material universe and the evolution and purpose of the human race.

Sherwood, Jane (1964) *Post-Mortem Journal. Communications from T.E. Lawrence* Neville Spearman London Reprinted (1976)

In the early years of Jane Sherwood's work as an automatic writing medium, three communicators helped her to build up a picture of after-death conditions and how they relate to life on earth. One of these three called himself 'Scott', a pseudonym which he asked to be used in any published work as he wished to preserve his anonymity. From the beginning of the communications in 1938, however, he had identified himself as T. E. Lawrence, or Lawrence of Arabia, who died in 1935. The material that came through from Lawrence helped in the writing of the two books *The Psychic Bridge* and *The Country Beyond,* and also provided the text for what appears here under the title of *Post-Mortem Journal,* a title suggested by Lawrence himself. He ceased communicating in 1959 and his personal account of the initial stages of life after death was published five years later. This very interesting account can perhaps best be summarised in the first paragraph of Chapter 5:

> "I begin now to get a wider notion of the whole process of development by which men move towards their own fulfilment. It is a vast and slow-moving progress and for a long while I could only see a small part of it. The expansion of outlook as the actual 'scheme of things' unfolds itself is gradual and inevitable. First comes the knowledge that life is indeed indestructible, then the stern experience that the soul goes inevitably to its own place, and, lastly, the realisation that no man is damned however he may be warped by evil but that by effort and suffering he can free himself from it and develop to the highest level of which he is capable."

Sherwood, Jane (1992) *Peter's Gate: A Book for the Elderly* **C.W. Daniel Saffron Walden Essex UK ISBN 0-85207-259-7** First published (1973) Churches' Fellowship for Psychical and Spiritual Studies

This wonderful little book of 87 pages, intended essentially for the elderly, is one which everyone could benefit from reading. Based on the author's researches and earlier writings, it is a simple, straightforward 'manual' to guide one through the later stages of life, the processes of dying and the opening up of a new life following the loss of the body. In thirteen short but vivid chapters, Jane Sherwood provides a wealth of practical spiritual guidance on coming to terms with life and death – on maturing inwardly and making one's soul ready in preparation for the transition which is death. A particularly useful aspect of the chapter on dying (Ch 10) are the four contrasting accounts of after-death experiences, based on information obtained during "half a lifetime's work as a medium".

Greaves, Helen (1969) *Testimony of Light* **World Fellowship Press Ltd. for The Churches' Fellowship of Psychical and Spiritual Studies**

Frances Banks "was an outstanding woman in many fields of endeavour" and a deeply spiritual person. For twenty-five years she was a Sister in an Anglican Community in South Africa, during which time she was the principal of a teachers' training college. She was the author of many books on psychology and similar subjects. Eventually, she left the community and, during the last eight years of her life, she and Helen Greaves worked together psychically and spiritually. Because of this close relationship, after her death in 1962, Frances Banks was able to communicate "by telepathy and inspiration" with Helen Greaves. This resulted in the series of scripts which have been published as *The Testimony of Light.* In the scripts, transmitted over a period of two years, she recounts her experience of death "...and the change into a new conception of living..." As Helen Greaves says "She gives us freely of her further knowledge of the progress of the soul outwards, upwards and forwards into Divinity." This book is a classic of communication across the barrier of death.

Frances Banks published her own last book in 1962, just before she died. It was an account of her researches into psychic and mystical phenomena and discusses many of the subjects associated with the survival of death. It is:

Banks, Frances (1962) *Frontiers of Revelation* Max Parrish London

Fifteen years after *The Testimony of Light* Helen Greaves published a sequel containing further communications from Frances Banks:

Greaves, Helen (1984) *The Challenging Light* Neville Spearman Sudbury Suffolk UK ISBN 85435-105-1

Greaves, Helen (1967) *The Dissolving Veil* James Clarke London. Published for The Churches Fellowship for Psychical and Spiritual Studies. Reprinted (1975) Neville Spearman London ISBN 0-85435-003-9

The Dissolving Veil is Helen Greaves' autobiography. In the first, main, part of the book she describes how, from childhood to maturity, she developed both psychically and spiritually and includes her own personal experiences of contact across the divide of death. The second part consists of a series of cases in which she was able to help individuals by developing contact with dead relatives on their behalf. Her experience with 'Moya' particularly is a remarkable story of real and purposeful communication with the dead. The very brief Introduction probably best sums up the contents of this book. It is:

> "These are my experiences. These are the evidences which have led me to believe in communications between the two worlds. This is the way I feel that God has led me.
>
> "I put them out for you to read. Perhaps they may strike an answering chord in your own life."

Greaves, Helen (1974) *The Wheel of Eternity* Neville Spearman London ISBN 0-85435-192-2 Reprinted (1995) [paperback] C.W. Daniel Saffron Walden Essex UK ISBN 0-85435-192-2

Helen Greaves describes how, because of her spiritual gifts, she was used

"...by Higher Powers as a means of bringing the light of understanding to earthbound souls imprisoned by their own ignorance and selfishness. Little did [she] realise, when she first came to live in [her] cottage, that she would be deeply and personally involved in an emotional, psychic and spiritual sense, in the life of a former inhabitant of the cottage, technically 'dead' but quite unaware of the fact, as are so many souls today.

"The story tells of a triangle of human relationships, with its roots in the tragic life of this world, and its dramatic working out of the consequences in the Shadow Lands of the next world. The arrogant, domineering mistress, hating her idiot bastard son, and enslaving and despising the old woman who was her maid, is the apex of a human triangle of love-hate relationships." (Rev K. G. Cuming in the Foreword)

This book is a valuable account of the interactions between how we live our lives in this world and the consequences we reap in the next world. It is an important source of information for those seeking to learn more about life after death.

Leslie Flint was probably the best known and most widely tested direct voice medium of recent times. He described his life and experiences in his autobiography:

Flint, Leslie (1971) *Voices in the Dark. My life as a medium* Macmillan London SBN 333-12201-1

Here we have a frank and detailed account of the life and development of a very gifted medium, from his early childhood up to his sixtieth year. He gives many accounts of his sittings with numerous people, from the lowest to the highest, and describes in detail the evidence he provided them with which convinced them of the survival of their 'dead' relatives. Often the communicating voices of the deceased entered into long and complex conversations with the sitters, where personal details known only to the individuals concerned were recounted between the living and the dead. He also describes the mechanism by which the apparently independent voices were produced and gives details of the tests which he underwent to check the reality of his gifts. He was never demonstrated to have been fraudulent in his communications.

Sandys, Cynthia (1986) *The Awakening Letters* **Selected and edited by Rosamond Lehmann. C.W. Daniel Saffron Walden Essex UK ISBN 0-850207-1779** Originally published (1978) Neville Spearman

A book of fascinating automatic writing by Cynthia Sandys with the spirit help of her daughter Patricia and Rosamond Lehmann's daughter Sally. It is a more substantial sequel to *Letters from our Daughters,* published earlier by the College of Psychic Studies in two small booklets. This book contains 'letters' from a variety of friends in Spirit, among them Wellesley Tudor Pole and Zed Adamski. They give fascinating information about the amazing possibilities in the afterlife, including space exploration and future development of our planet.

Lehmann, Rosamond (1982) *The Swan in the Evening. Fragments of an inner life* **Virago Press London ISBN 0-86068-299-4** Originally published (1967) Collins

Rosamond Lehmann published eight novels and is one of the most distinguished British writers of the last century. In this autobiography she recreates her childhood and the experiences which made her the woman she became, moving on to tell of the birth of her beloved daughter Sally and the tragedy of Sally's death at the age of twenty-four. But the real purpose of the book is to relate the totally unexpected psychic and mystical experiences she underwent after that terrible loss. The meaning of such events, their message of hope and comfort to others, she then passes on through a letter to her granddaughter.

Praagh, James Van (1999) *Reaching to Heaven. A spiritual journey through life and death* **Judy Piatkus London ISBN 0-7499-1995-7** Originally published in USA by Dutton/Penguin.

A well known American medium James Van Praagh has written a down-to-earth guide to what happens to the individual at death and afterwards. He describes what the spirit world is like, how a soul chooses to be reborn and how the process of reincarnation works. *Reaching to Heaven* is based on many years of communicating with discarnate souls on behalf of those left behind.

Hamilton-Parker, Craig (2001) *What to Do When You Are Dead. Living better in the afterlife* Sterling Publishing Co. Inc. New York USA ISBN 0-8069-2996-0

In spite of the somewhat incongruous title, this book is of considerable value particularly to those beginning an exploration of the concept of the afterlife. The author, a successful mental medium, uses his own extensive experience combined with material from many other sources to paint a picture of what happens to the individual at death and afterwards. There is also an extensive introductory section describing the spiritual background to the remainder of the book.

Although all the topics covered are only dealt with fairly superficially, and there are many other more detailed accounts in the older literature, nevertheless it makes a useful startingpoint for the newcomer to this field. Its main weakness, perhaps, is the lack of any bibliography for further reading.

A number of very recent books have been written by well known American mediums. Several of these have been reviewed by Professor Gary Schwartz in his book *The Afterlife Experiments* in a section of recommended readings entitled "The Art of Mediumship: Personal and Professional" (see p 30). An important aspect of these works is that, with one exception, they were all written by mediums whose abilities have been clearly demonstrated in the experiments described in Professor Schwartz's book. The following brief reviews of these books are reprinted here with the permission of Professor Schwartz.

Smith, Susy (2001) *The Afterlife Codes. Searching for evidence of the survival of the soul* Hampton Roads Charlottsville VA USA ISBN 1-57174-191-7

Truly inspirational, this book tells the life story of Susy Smith, the "matriarch of survival research." Smith shows how it is possible for skeptical laypersons (herself and others) to develop the capacity to make contact with deceased love ones and test the communications for authenticity. Her thirteenth book, published shortly before she died, includes a detailed description of her remarkable afterlife codes experiment, offering a $10,000 reward for anyone who correctly receives her secret code.

Rothchild, Joel (2001) *Signals: An inspiring story of life after life* New World Library Novato CA USA ISBN 1-57731-179-5

Rothchild is a medical miracle. He is the longest surviving person with AIDS. His book describes how after his dear friend Albert died of AIDS, Rothchild received repeated and compelling afterlife communications that provide strong evidence for life after death. The style of writing beautifully complements his inspiring story of the possibility of love and life-sustaining support from the other side.

Dalzell, George (2002) *Messages: Evidence for life after death* **Hampton Roads Charlottsville VA USA**

This is the third recommended book that documents how any person can potentially become a "lay scientist" and obtain strong evidence for life after death. Dalzell is a psychiatric social worker who, after the death of his dear friend Michael, discovered that he was receiving repeated and compelling after-death communications that could be documented definitively through contact with mediums. Dalzell has become a research medium who collaborates with the Human Energy Systems Laboratory at the University of Arizona.

Edward, John (2000) *One Last Time: A psychic medium speaks to those we have loved and lost* **Berkley New York USA ISBN 0-42516-692-9**

Edward participated in three experiments in the Human Energy Systems Laboratory. His profound talents are demonstrated weekly on his successful television series, *Crossing Over with John Edward.* Edward's book is essential reading for people interested in the art of mediumship and integrity in living.

Northrop, Susan with McLoughlin, Kate (1996) *Séance: Healing messages from beyond* **Dell Books New York USA ISBN 0-44022-176-5**

Northrop is another remarkable medium who participated in three experiments at the University of Arizona. Her life story is powerful. She has lived with scorn, ridicule and prejudice, yet continues to practice what she knows to be true through repeated experience. Northrop is outspoken about the reality of mediumship and its significance. Her book presents a striking and comforting vision of the power of mind to connect the visible with the living invisible.

Anderson, George and Barone, Andrew (2000) *Lessons from the Light: Extraordinary messages of comfort and hope from the other side* **Berkley New York USA ISBN 0-41517-416-6**

George Anderson is one of the world's most distinguished and well studied mediums. A deeply spiritual person, whose primary purpose is to bring through messages of love and forgiveness, he is also devoted to obtaining information that can be validated empirically. Anderson was one of the members of the "dream team" in the HBO experiment conducted at the University of Arizona. His book is moving and profoundly meaningful.

Betty Shine There are many books by people who are both mediums and healers but those by Betty Shine are suggested here because she has gifts and experiences even more extraordinary than usual in her field. The books are easy reading and full of remarkable stories of clairvoyance and healing. Betty is described as cheerful, down-to-earth and full of humour; she has the clairvoyant ability to diagnose medically. She is able to see the inner three layers of the aura, the energy field around the body, in which, she says, disease manifests before physical problems become apparent. Betty Shine also describes a system of training she has devised for developing "mind energy" in a positive way.

Shine, Betty (1989) *Mind to Mind. The secrets of your mind energy revealed* **Bantam Press London ISBN 0-593-01525-6**

Shine, Betty (1991) *Mind Magic. The key to the universe* **Corgi Books London ISBN 0-552-13671-9**

7 The Experiences of Doctors, Scientists and Others in the Study of Death and Dying

In virtually all cultures throughout history there has been an interest, indeed sometimes even a seeming obsession, with what happens at death and in the afterlife. Particularly in the case of the rulers and other important persons, ancient cultures often went to great lengths to ensure that the spirits of their dead had a smooth passage and were well supported in the next world. The best known example is that of the Egyptian Pharaohs, but many others have been discovered by archeological research. Perhaps the best account of what was believed about the after-life in ancient times is:

Budge, E. A. Wallis (1967) *The Egyptian Book of the Dead* **Dover Publications New York USA**

This is a detailed account of the ancient Egyptians' understanding of the processes of death and the after-life. "This book is simply a detailed description of a near-death experience. It starts with a judgement scene and goes on to reveal many gods and various voices, continues on a long boat trip through a dark tunnel, and ends with union with a bright light."

A new translation and commentary which has been recently produced is:

Seleem, Ramses (2001) *The Illustrated Egyptian Book of the Dead* **Godsfield Press Ltd. Newton Abbot Devon UK ISBN 1-84181-109-2**

In a rather different context, there is the Tibetan Buddhist account of the passage through death and after which was originally published as:

Evans-Wentz, W.Y. (1957) *The Tibetan Book of the Dead. Or the after-death experiences on the bardo plane* **3rd ed Oxford University Press Oxford UK**

More recent translations of this text are found in:

Thurman, Robert, (1993) *The Tibetan Book of the Dead* **Bantam Books New York USA ISBN 0-553370-90-1 Also published by Thorsons London ISBN 1-85538-412-4**

And:

Freemantle, Francesca and Trungpa, Chogyam (2000) *The Tibetan Book of the Dead* **Shambhala Classics London ISBN 1-57062-747-9**

Probably the most 'reader-friendly' translation and interpretation of this classic is:

Hodge, Stephen with Boord, Martin (1999) *The Illustrated Tibetan Book of the Dead. A new translation with commentary* **Thorsons London ISBN 0-7225-3754-9**

"*The Tibetan Book of the Dead* gives the dying person control over his own death and rebirth. The Tibetans, who believed in reincarnation, felt that the dying person could influence his own destiny. It was meant to be read *after* death to help the deceased find the right path."

Another, similar, early account of the death process coming from Central America is *The Aztec Song of the Dead* which tells the story of the god and legendary king Quetzalcoatl. This work "served to enlighten the Aztecs about the world beyond." (The above three quotations have been taken from Morse with Perry, *Closer to the Light* (see p 43)).

The classical text of *The Tibetan Book of the Dead* has been reinterpreted and updated in:

Rinpoche, Sogyal (1992) *The Tibetan Book of Living and Dying* **Rider Books London ISBN 0-7126-5437-2 Also (1992) HarperCollins New York USA**

This is a book about living and dying because, "…in the Buddhist approach, life and death are seen as one whole, where death is the beginning of another chapter of life." The continuity of life from birth to rebirth is seen here as the continuation of mind or consciousness, rather than relating to a specific entity like the soul as envisaged by western tradition. Sogyal Rinpoche provides us with a comprehensive guide describing in modern terms "…the majestic vision of life and death that underlies the Tibetan tradition…" and shows how we may undertake a range of practices which will transform our lives, prepare us for death and enable us to help those who are dying.

A useful introduction to the beliefs about death and concepts of the afterlife as found in many religions and cultures is contained in:

Grof, Stanislav and Grof, Christina (1990) *Beyond Death. The gates of consciousness* **Thames & Hudson London ISBN 0-500-81019-2** First published (1980) Thames & Hudson

The authors provide a summary review of the place of death and what follows from Christian, Jewish, Moslem, ancient Greek, Persian, Egyptian, East Indian, Tibetan and Pre-Columbian societies, with particular reference to the Egyptian and Tibetan Books of the Dead. The text is accompanied by numerous pictures illustrating the beliefs of these cultures.

Sir William Barrett From quite early on in the development of psychical research there was an interest in, and the collection of, accounts of death-bed experiences. Sir William Barrett was someone who was involved in this area amongst his other interests. Barrett was another famous physicist, like Sir William Crookes and Sir Oliver Lodge, who became involved in investigating psychic phenomena. As a young professor in Dublin in 1874 he took part in some experiments on hypnosis, with remarkable results. He followed this up with further work on telepathy. In spite of the very negative scientific attitude to such research at the time, he was intellectually honest enough to realise that here was a significant field of work which needed to be investigated. Whilst staying in London in late 1881 he suggested the idea of founding a society of scientists and philosophers who would investigate open-mindedly psychic phenomena. He organised meetings which, in February 1882, led to the founding of the Society for Psychical Research. As Colin Wilson emphasises, Barrett "...was dragged into belief in 'the paranormal' against his will – even against his better judgement." He tried to find scientific explanations for the range of psychic phenomena which he and others were witnessing all the time, but was unable to do so along orthodox scientific lines. Towards the end of his life he admitted that his work had brought him to the point where he believed in a spiritual world and in life after death.

Barrett's interest in the fact that many people at the point of death appear to see their dead relatives led him to collect authenticated examples of such appearances with the intention of publishing a book on the subject. Unfortunately he died before the manuscript was finished but it was edited and published posthumously as:

Barrett, Sir William (1926) *Death-Bed Visions* **Methuen London** Republished as:

Barrett, Sir William (1986) *Death-Bed Visions. The psychic experiences of the dying* With an introduction by Colin Wilson **Aquarian Press Wellingborough Northants UK. The Colin Wilson Library of the Paranormal**

As Colin Wilson states: "In spite of its shortness, this is one of the most remarkable and original contributions to psychical research ever published." "...it undoubtedly deserves its place as one of the great classics of psychical research." Although some of the examples of visions seen by the dying could be (and are) dismissed as being simply hallucinations, this explanation became more difficult in those cases where the dying person was unaware that the relative seen was already dead. This collection of mainly well authenticated cases was the result of collaboration between Barrett and his wife, a surgeon, who had considerable experience of the dying.

A much more recent, although very similar, account of death-bed visions has been published as:

Osis, Karlis and Haraldsson, Erlendur (1977) *At the Hour of Death* **Hastings House Norwalk CT USA 3rd edition (1997) ISBN 0-8038-9386-8** The publisher of this book has also sometimes been quoted as Avon Books New York USA

At the Hour of Death is an account of the work of two researchers who surveyed death-bed experiences in America and India. In spite of considerable cultural differences between the populations, the death-bed visions were found to be remarkably similar. Although the majority of dying people drift into unconsciousness before death, a significant minority remain clearly conscious to the end and these individuals often have transformative experiences of serenity, peace and elation. They no longer have any fear of death and may believe that they are being met by dead relatives. This scientifically rigorous study, based on the observations of more than a thousand doctors and nurses, concludes:

> "…that this evidence strongly suggests life after death – more strongly than any alternative hypothesis can explain the data. Neither medical, nor psychological, nor cultural conditioning can explain away deathbed visions. Moreover, they are relatively independent of age, sex, education, religion, and socioeconomic status. Taken in conjunction with other evidence obtained by competent research into this question … we feel that the total body of information makes possible a fact based, rational, and therefore realistic belief in life after death."

In the West there has been an increasing interest in the study of the processes of death and dying during the past 50 years or more. This development has largely been undertaken by doctors, scientists and others with a professional interest in what happens to the individual during the time of death – and in the periods before and after death. It has resulted among these professionals in a growing awareness of the likelihood of the continuity of individual consciousness from this life into further life beyond death; a possibility which their original scientific training completely excluded. It has also resulted in a vast literature on the subjects of death and dying. What follows is a sample of the literature that has appeared in the past 30 years.

The *doyenne* of the science of thanatology – the study of death and dying – is Dr Elisabeth Kübler-Ross [sometimes spelt Elizabeth] whose many books have opened up what, a few decades ago, was for most people a taboo subject. She has also been prepared boldly to state her conclusions, gained through many years of the study of the experiences of thousands of dying people. These are that death is not the end of everything, but that we do consciously survive the death of our bodies in full retention of our faculties. Dr Kübler-Ross' seminal book is:

Kübler-Ross, Elisabeth (1989) *On Death and Dying.* **Tavistock Publications London ISBN 0-422-75490-0** First published (1969) and has appeared in several editions since.

This and the following book are essentially psychology or social science texts written largely for professionals and, as such, may not be easy reading for everyone.

Kübler-Ross, Elisabeth (1993) *Questions and Answers on Death and Dying* **Collier Macmillan New York USA ISBN 0-02-089142-3** First published (1974) Collier Macmillan New York ISBN 0-025671-20-0

Kübler-Ross, Elisabeth, editor (1986) *Death, the Final Stage of Growth* **Simon & Schuster London ISBN 0-671-62238-2** First published (1975) Prentice-Hall Englewood Cliffs New Jersey USA ISBN 0-131970-12-7

In the introduction, Dr Kübler-Ross states that, among other things, the "…book attempts to familiarize the reader with [many] aspects of death and dying, with the viewpoints of other people, other cultures, other religions, and philosophies…" and in particular it covers the Jewish, Buddhist and Hindu approaches to death. The final four pages, entitled Omega, contain many spiritually oriented passages such as "Death is the final stage of growth in this life. There is no total death. Only the body dies. The self or spirit…is eternal." And, "Death…may be viewed as the curtain between the existence that we are conscious of and one that is hidden from us until we raise that curtain."

Kübler-Ross, Elisabeth (1991) *On Life After Death* **Celestial Arts Berkeley California USA ISBN 0-89087-653-3**

This short book (82 pages) is a collection of four essays which summarises her many "years of 'working with the dying and learning from them what life is all about,' in-depth research on life after death, and her own feelings and opinions about this fascinating and controversial subject." Three of the four essays – *Living and Dying, There is no Death,* and *Life, Death and Life After Death* – are particularly appropriate to the subject of survival.

Kübler-Ross, Elisabeth (1997) *The Wheel of Life. A memoir of living and dying* **Bantam Press London ISBN 0-593-04302-2** Originally published (1997) Scribner New York USA ISBN 0-684-19361-2

The Wheel of Life is Dr Kübler-Ross's autobiography. In it she "traces the events that shaped her intellectually and spiritually, and inevitably led her to explain her ultimate truth – that death does not exist but is a transformation."

Dr Sukie Miller is a psychotherapist who has undertaken extensive research into the attitudes in many cultures worldwide toward life after death. As she states in the introduction to her book *After Death,* from her studies she "…knew that almost every culture throughout history encompassed in its belief system an idea of the afterdeath. Wide reading on the subject brought me into contact with detailed landscapes, even finely drawn maps of landscapes beyond life as we know it." Her book seeks to address the important question – "What happens to us *after* we die?" – and her extensive cross-cultural research identifies four distinct stages of the afterdeath journey:

> stage 1 is the waiting place where the dead individual is transformed from a physical to a spiritual being;
>
> stage 2 is the judgement phase where some form of judgement takes place and the individual's future is determined;
>
> stage 3 is the realm of possibilities where the individual enjoys, or suffers, the results of the judgement; and
>
> stage 4 is the return, or rebirth, where the individual returns to life in the physical world with a new body and personality. Her studies also help us to understand that with peoples who live in close contact with their dead the border between life and death is highly permeable; there is often no border at all.

Miller, Sukie (1998) *After Death. How people around the world map the journey after life* **Touchstone New York USA ISBN 0-684-83869-9** Originally published (1997) Simon & Schuster New York ISBN 0-684-82236-9

Another individual who, like Dr Kübler-Ross, has worked for many years with dying patients is Kathleen Dowling Singh. Her experiences as a hospice nurse, combined with her own Buddhist philosophy, have led her to write the following:

Singh, Kathleen Dowling (1999) *The Grace in Dying. How we are transformed spiritually as we die* **Newleaf Dublin Eire ISBN 0-7171-2873-3**

"In this remarkable book Kathleen Dowling Singh offers us a rich and rewarding path to understanding the process of dying. She helps us to see death as safe and natural – a stage of enlightenment, of finally coming home to our true self. Examining the end of life in the light of current psychological understanding, religious wisdom and compassionate medical science, she offers a fresh, deeply comforting message of hope and courage as we contemplate the meaning of our mortality. With profound insight, she balances expert analysis with moving accounts drawn from her experience working with hundreds of dying patients at a large hospice.

Written for those aware that life is coming to an end, those who care for the dying and, ultimately, for all of us who inevitably face our own death and the deaths of the people we love, *The Grace in Dying* reveals that dying is the most transforming and spiritually enriching of life's experiences."

Rees, Dewi (2001) *Death and Bereavement. The psychological, religious and cultural interfaces* **Whurr Publishers London 2nd edition ISBN 1-86156-223-3**

Death and Bereavement is essentially a textbook giving a comprehensive account of the psychology of death and bereavement, written by the former director of St. Mary's Hospice, Birmingham. Nevertheless, it is written in a very readable style and provides much information which is pertinent to the subject of this bibliography.

The early chapters (Chs 2 - 8) give an overview, across the world, of attitudes and beliefs on death and the afterlife from religions great and small, old and new; showing that "Running like a connecting thread through all religions is a steadfast belief in the existence of an afterlife." There is also a great deal on related subjects such as funeral rites and mourning customs.

The final chapters (Chs 22 - 24) deal with:

1 The phenomenon of the sense of the presence of the dead often felt by the recently bereaved and recounts, here and in the Appendix, the author's own work on investigating this subject;

2 A chapter reviewing the Near-Death Experience; and,

3 "The Significance of Death", the author's summing up of the significance of the widespread belief in life after death.

In between these first and last sections is much useful material on the themes of dying, death and bereavement. The whole is fully referenced and indexed.

Guggenheim, Bill and Guggenheim, Judy (1995) *Hello from Heaven!* **Thorsons London ISBN 0-7225-3397-7 Also published (1999) Bantam Books New York USA ISBN 0-55357-643-8**

In *Hello from Heaven!* the authors have produced "the first complete study of an exciting new field of research called After-Death Communication, or ADC". Over a period of seven years they examined and collected more than 3,300 first-hand experiences from people from all walks of life; experiences which – apparently initiated by a deceased loved one – occurred directly to the individual without the help of a medium. The 'communications' included sensing a presence, hearing a voice, feeling a touch, smelling a fragrance, seeing a partial or full appearance, physical phenomena and symbolic communication. The book is based on 350 accounts selected to provide an in-depth study of the twelve most common types of after-death contacts. Using comprehensive interviews the Guggenheims have produced a scientific study of ADCs which strongly suggests the reality of these experiences.

Martin, Joel and Romanowski, Patricia (1998) *Love Beyond Life. The healing power of after-death communications* **Bantam Books New York USA ISBN 0-440-22649-X Also published (1998) Dell Publishing New York. Same ISBN**

Love Beyond Life is another study of after-death communications similar to that of the Guggenheims above. The book is based on a collection of hundreds of cases of ADCs which was originally triggered off by what came up on a radio talk show hosted by Martin. As Gary Schwartz says: "Written for the general public, it reviews research and personal experiences about the role that afterlife communications can play in healing from grief. The authors' focus is on the enduring motivation of love…" Martin and Romanowski have also written three books about the work of the well-known American medium George Anderson (see p 81). These are:

We Don't Die: George Anderson's conversations with the other side (1988)

We are Not Forgotten: George Anderson's messages of hope from the other side (1991)

Our Children Forever: Messages from children on the other side (1994)

Wright, Sylvia Hart (2002) *When Spirits Come Calling. The open-minded skeptic's guide to after-death contacts* **Blue Dolphin Publishing Nevada City CA USA ISBN 1-57733-095-1**

Sylvia Hart Wright was an academic who had no interest or belief in the paranormal until her husband died. Following this, she experienced a number of significant events which suggested contacts from her dead husband. These led her to research the field and to undertake many in-depth interviews with others who apparently had also had spontaneous after-death communications. *When Spirits Come Calling* recounts a series of these ADCs which are used to illustrate a wide-ranging study and discussion of the subjects of death, dying and communication with the dead. This study brought about a total change in her own attitude towards death. As she says: "Over time, my own experiences, plus scores of interviews with people who've had similar ones, have transformed me from a total skeptic to a firm believer in survival of the spirit after death."

Morse, Don (2000) *Searching for Eternity: A scientist's spiritual journey to overcome death anxiety* **Eagle Wing Books Memphis TN USA ISBN 0-940829-27-4**

Dr Morse, a highly qualified academic, originally believed in the absolute finality of death. However, following illness, a near-death experience and several unexpected family deaths, he was prompted to set out on a quest to determine what humanity, and particularly science, knew about the nature of death and what – if anything – happens after death. In particular, he hoped to overcome his anxiety about death, which he faced. His subsequent spiritual journey led him to review the literature about religion, mysticism, cosmology, NDEs, OBEs, apparitions, visions dreams, past-life regression, mediumistic communication and related subjects. He also conducted many interviews with people with relevant experiences. In *Searching for Eternity* he summarises and assesses the vast amount of data and research which he reviewed, together with the history of belief in an after-life from past and present religions, and comes to the, to him inescapable, conclusion that an after-life does exist and that death is just a transition to a greater reality. It is an impressive and convincing study.

୬

Davies, Brenda (2002) *Journey of the Soul. Awakening ourselves to the enduring cycle of life* **Hodder Mobius London ISBN 0-340-73389-6**

Dr Davies is both a consultant psychiatrist and a spiritual healer who, using her extensive knowledge and experience, has sought in *Journey of the Soul* to put human life into a wider context than the brief physical existence that many consider to be all there is. As she says: "This is a book about the endless journey of the soul – that spiral of evolution from our inception billions of years ago to that moment long from now when we will once again reunite with whatever we know as the Source..." and "Our soul is on a journey which began eons ago and which, for most of us, will continue for centuries yet."

The book is divided into two parts, the earthly phase of human life – covering birth, physical life and death; and that phase taking place on the soul plane following death and leading to rebirth. The second part is of greater interest here, as it deals in some detail with what is known about the after-death experience. Nevertheless, it is written essentially as a whole, integrating the concept of spiritual growth and development in both phases into the central theme of the 'journey of the soul'". Each chapter finishes with valuable affirmation and meditation exercises and the whole is well illustrated by examples of past-life regressions taken from the author's own practice.

୬

Freke, Timothy (2002) *In the Light of Death. Spiritual insight to help you live with death and bereavement* **Godsfield Press Alresford Hants UK ISBN 1-84181-169-6**

This book does not set out to provide evidence for the survival of death. Instead, it is an inspiring and thoughtful exploration of the greatest of life's mysteries – that it ends in death – based on the wisdom of the perennial philosophy. It thus provides a deeply spiritual basis for an understanding of the interrelationship between life and death as expounded by the world's great mystical traditions. As such it complements other, more factual, studies.

୬

8 Personal Experiences of Ordinary Individuals

There are also a number of accounts of the experiences of individuals who, without any apparent psychic gifts or other 'advantages', underwent such extensive involvements across the boundaries of death that they decided to publish an account of their experiences. Some of these books are included below:

Kennedy, David (1973) *A Venture in Immortality* **Colin Smythe Gerrards Cross Bucks UK ISBN 0-900-67579-9**

A careful and readable account of communication between the author, a Minister in the Church of Scotland, and his wife who died prematurely. A fascinating and convincing record.

෨

Pearce, Ian (1986) *One Man's Odyssey* **C.W. Daniel Co. Saffron Walden Essex UK ISBN 0-85207-179-5**

Dr Ian Pearce was a 'perfectly normal, orthodox doctor' in Diss, Norfolk, until the death, from leukaemia, of his darling daughter Vicky, ten years old. His grief started him on a spiritual journey which put him in touch with Vicky and the reality of the Afterlife, and made him a healer and pioneer of holistic cancer care. His communications with Vicky, and later with 'Paul', through a medium, are transcribed from tapes.

෨

Two recently published books recount the experiences of mothers who, having lost young sons, sought for evidence that they had survived in the spirit world. They recount the evidence that convinced them of their sons' survival; Gwen Byrne's descriptions of the materialisation evidence that she witnessed over a long period of time are particularly interesting.

Byrne, Gwen (1994) *Russell* **Janus Publishing Co. ISBN 1-85756-150-3**

Prentice, Margaret (1999) *Richard, Spirit and I* **Lionheart Press No ISBN**

෨

Richelieu, Peter (1996) *A Soul's Journey* **Thorsons London ISBN 0-7225-3291-1**
Originally published (1953) also Turnstone Press Wellingborough Northants UK (1972) ISBN 0-85500-065-1

"While in a state of despair after the death of his brother, the author is visited by Acharya, an Indian mystic. Using astral projection, Acharya takes him out of the physical world onto the astral planes of the 'afterlife'. Each astral plane teaches something new about life and death, karma and the ego. Through a series of meetings with the 'dead' – including his brother – the author comes to realize how irrational it is to fear death.

Through his teaching, Acharya opens up a whole vision of life in the world that follows this, a world where anything is possible.

Based on notes taken immediately following out-of-body experiences, this book is both enlightening and absorbing. It gives the reader a direct insight into the unknown mysteries of life and death."

Rose, Aubrey (1997) *Journey into Immortality. The story of David Rose* **Lennard Publishing Harpenden Herts UK ISBN 1-85291-133-6**

This is the story, written by his father, of a remarkable young man who died of cancer at the age of twenty-three. During David's illness he had received help from healers but they were unable to effect a cure. After his death David's father was guided to the direct voice medium Leslie Flint and soon made contact with his [Aubrey's] father-in-law and then with David. Communication was not always easy but, as Aubrey Rose says, "the sittings continued, the messages mounted, the tape recorders continued to whirl, and the joy of being once again with David uplifted us as we had confirmation after confirmation that death was not the end."

9 The Survival of Pets and Other Animals

t has been generally assumed that animals do not have specific souls which survive death as do individual human beings, but that after death the spiritual ife force that activates animals returns to a 'general pool' at a higher level. However, there is evidence that more intelligent animals such as dogs, cats and horses, particularly those which have lived in close proximity to people as pets, may also survive death as individual entities. There are a few books which deal specifically with this subject, such as:

Barbanell, Sylvia (1940) *What happens when your animal dies* Spiritualist Press London ISBN [of later printing] 0-85437-014-5 Republished (2002) Spiritual Truth Foundation The CoachHouse Stanstead Hall Stanstead Essex CM24 8UD

This little book was first published in 1940 and has been reprinted frequently ever since. There is a huge volume of evidence for animal survival and the writer presents in clear, simple, commonsense language many and varied instances of the return and presence of "dead" animals. Over the years this book has been of great comfort to those who have lost animal friends.

But I say unto you, That Elias is come already...
Then the disciples understood that
he spake unto them of John the Baptist.

Jesus. Matthew xvii, 12-13

❧

As one of their leading dogmas they [the Druids]
inculcate this:
That souls are not annihilated,
but pass after death from one body to another.

Caesar. De Bello Gallico, vi, 14

❧

All souls are subjected to the test of transmigration...
Souls must in the end be plunged back into
the substance from which they came.
But before this happens, they must have developed
all the perfections the germs of which are implanted within them.

The Zohar (Jewish)

Discussion

The material in this bibliography consists essentially of a list of books and other sources together with some description and a linking commentary; it does not describe in any detail the evidence contained in these sources. Nevertheless, for anyone who is prepared to read with an open mind and to assess the available evidence, it should become clear that the case for survival is a strong one[1] [See pp 123-127 for all references]

A large proportion of the evidence in favour of this concept has been obtained through the activities of mediums or sensitives, gifted individuals who appear to have the ability to cross the 'barrier' between the material and spiritual worlds and, in a number of ways, to act as channels for information passing between these two worlds. Even so, in spite of the fact that many of the best mediums have been investigated and validated by psychic researchers, there remain those people who, often suspicious of anything to do with the paranormal, hesitate to accept such evidence.

However, there is also much evidence coming from other, equally sound, sources not associated with mediums (e.g. NDEs, reincarnation research, ITCs) which supports the integrity and reliability of the main mass of material. Thus, the various sources of evidence come together to produce a realistic and consistent body of material which strongly supports survival.

The survival conclusion

This conclusion has also been arrived at by many individuals, frequently scientifically qualified and experienced, who have gone to the trouble to undertake research themselves, or to investigate the evidence thoroughly. Examples of these individuals who have been prepared to speak out – often through the printed word – concerning the reliability of the evidence are:

Sir William Crookes,

Professor Charles Richet,

Dr Glen Hamilton,

Dr Raynor Johnson,

Professor Arthur Ellison **and**

Dr Victor Zammit –

who is one of the most recent and most outspoken supporters of the evidence based reality of survival, and who has drawn attention to the fact that much of the available evidence would be accepted by legal jurisdictions around the world as being proven beyond reasonable doubt (p 10)

Although a great deal of the evidence has been criticised, and even 'deconstructed', by sceptically minded individuals there remain several cases, or bodies of research, which have withstood all but the most unreasonable criticisms of their validity. Examples of these, and of individual mediums whose professional integrity has never been successfully criticised, are:

1 The Cross-Correspondences (p 16) A 30-year series of communications, involving multiple mediums and fragmented, abstruse material, of such complexity that the only reasonable conclusion applicable is that they originated from the mind of the 'dead' F.W.H. Myers.

2 The Proxy Sittings (p 24) The best known series of sittings with mediums designed to prevent telepathic communication between medium and sitter is that of the Rev. Charles Drayton Thomas' 20-year series with Mrs. Osborne Leonard.

3 Sir William Crookes (p 13) Crookes' critical researches, particularly with the famous physical medium Daniel D. Home and the materialisation medium Florence Cook, are among the best examples of carefully controlled psychical research.

4 Mrs. Leonora Piper (p 105) Mrs. Piper was one of the truly great mediums of the early years of psychical research. She was extensively investigated by Professor William James, Professor James Hyslop, Professor Richard Hodgson and Sir Oliver Lodge, all of whom became fully convinced of the reality of her mediumistic abilities.

5 Carlos Mirabelli (1899-1951), a Brazilian who was probably the most remarkable physical medium in recent history. He produced a range of physical phenomena even greater than those of D.D.Home. In particular, he was able to produce full materialisations of recently deceased people under test conditions – often in full daylight. His abilities were well attested by numerous critical witnesses, from a former President of Brazil downwards, but he was never fully investigated by researchers from the Society of Psychical Research or its American counterpart and thus his abilities have often been rejected by critics[2]

6 Individual cases. There are many individual cases reported in the research records which provide support for the concept of survival. Some of the best known of these are the Chaffin will case, the Samuel Bull (Ramsbury) case and the R101 disaster case.

There are also examples of more recent research which are equally sound and substantiated, such as:

7 **The Scole Report** (p 27) An extensive series of sittings, overseen by experienced psychic investigators, where most of the complex physical phenomena observed were only explainable on the basis of interaction between the sitters, the mediums and discarnate intelligences.

8 **The Afterlife Experiments** (p 30) The most recent and some of the best experiments carefully designed to test the validity of the medium/ sitter relationship as a true contact with the dead. They gave results strongly favouring the survival hypothesis.

In support of survival

Examples of indirect evidence supporting the case for survival which are not easily criticised because of their scientific integrity are:

the reincarnation research work of Professor Ian Stevenson (Section 3(a) p 33), and

much of the research into near-death experiences (Section 3(b) p 40).

It is possible to explain some apparently paranormal phenomena on the basis of normal, physical (or fraudulent) mechanisms. It is also possible to explain some apparent evidence for survival as the result of simple paranormal interactions between individuals which have nothing to do with discarnate spirits.

As Arthur Ellison (see p 1) warns, the basic paranormal phenomena of telepathy, psychokinesis, clairvoyance and precognition are now widely accepted as real aspects of human experience and it may be that some of the evidence for survival can be explained by direct telepathic contact between the medium and the sitter. Information about a deceased relative may be picked up subconsciously by the medium from the mind of the sitter and then be accepted as evidence of survival by the latter.

Super-psi or Super-ESP

Telepathic contact between medium and sitter has been widened by some commentators to include what has been termed "Super-psi" [the preferred expression] or "Super-ESP", the ability of the medium's mind to seek and find information from almost any source in the world, even when the medium has no conscious awareness of such information or sources, to explain away a wider range of survival evidence.

The hypothesis of Super-psi has been examined and apparently discredited by psychologist Allan Gauld in his book[3] *Mediumship and Survival*. There seems to be little direct evidence to support such a theory; certainly no serious attempt appears to have been made to test Super-psi as a genuine working hypothesis, which is essential if the concept is to be taken seriously.

Most recently an American philosopher and psychic researcher, Professor Stephen Braude, has suggested that Super-psi could well be a more logical explanation for much (but not all) of the apparent evidence for survival than is the concept of survival itself. This has generated an active discussion between Braude and other parapsychologists[4].

Professor Braude has considered the subject of survival and Super-psi in a number of recent publications[5], pointing out that there are good philosophical reasons for the Super-psi hypothesis to be taken much more seriously as an alternative explanation for many cases otherwise considered to support survival. He criticises many authors for underestimating the enormity of the theoretical challenges faced when seeking to demonstrate the reality of survival. Nevertheless, he believes that when all the alternative, non-survival, possibilities have been explored, there remain some cases which give us good reason for believing in life after death.

In seeking to refute the concept of survival, sceptics resort to a considerable variety of 'normal' mechanisms with which to explain the observations that have been recorded from sources of both direct and indirect evidence. Such explanatory hypotheses vary widely from psychological, physiological and biochemical mechanisms to straightforward hallucinations, delusions or fraud. They do not appear to have any single explanation which adequately covers all the observations associated with the survival hypothesis which have been described.

Occam's Razor

There is an important principle of both philosophy and science which needs to be applied on all occasions when an explanation is being sought for newly acquired material. It is called Occam's Razor. William of Occam (c 1280-1349) put forward the principle that, in seeking to solve a problem or to explain new data, it is necessary to find the simplest and most economic solution. Any new hypothesis should cover all the facts in the simplest manner.

When Occam's principle is applied to explaining the material described in this bibliography, it is clear that the survival hypothesis provides by far the simplest and most economical solution, whilst covering all the details. The survival hypothesis can be stated very simply as:

The primary reality in any human individual is spiritual and consists of an eternal soul, which manifests in the world in a physical body. The soul survives the death of the body, continuing to exist in the spiritual world, but may return many times to undertake further lives in other bodies. Contact between incarnate and discarnate entities, though difficult, has been well demonstrated.

This hypothesis not only provides an explanation for, but also brings together and unifies, all the often disparate phenomena associated with psychical/survival research. There does not appear to be any similar simple, unifying explanation for all this material available to the critics of survival. Indeed, as already mentioned, there appear to be many different theories to explain the wide range of phenomena. And, as Colin Wilson has said, "...the explanations are becoming absurdly complicated, and they violate the principle...[of]...Occam's razor"[6].

The Establishment's attitude to survival

The concept of our survival of death remains for many people, even after 150 years of often successful investigation, a subject which is ignored, if not ridiculed. The possible reasons for this are many, but one of the main reasons must directly relate to the response of the scientific and intellectual communities in Europe and America to the renewal of interest in psychic matters that began in the middle of the 19th century. 'Establishment' attitudes and responses to this renewal were almost entirely negative and often of an unscientific nature, and such attitudes have remained at the forefront of mainstream psychical research ever since. Because of the importance of these attitudes and reactions in influencing the way the media and the public have responded and continue to respond to the concept of survival, this subject is examined at some length[7].

Historical and scientific attitudes towards survival

Historically, attitudes concerning the survival of death have varied considerably. In the Middle Ages almost everyone believed in the primacy of a spiritual reality – God was the centre of all things *and* they also believed in a continuation of life after death. Following death, the soul either went to heaven or to hell and thus most people's chief concern was to save their souls in the next world. Knowledge of truth and reality was handed down by religious authority and was essentially fixed. Towards the end of the Middle Ages things began to change and several important events occurred. These were: the Renaissance (c. 1350 to 1600); the Reformation (the 16th century); the Scientific Revolution (15th 16th and 17th centuries); and the Enlightenment (17th and 18th centuries). In the Scientific Revolution, the ancient Greek view of science and nature was replaced by a new view. Nature and the universe began to be regarded as a machine rather than an organism. The experimental method – seeking specific answers to specific questions – was developed and it was decided that science should only investigate phenomena which could be weighed and measured. These changes were disastrous, since they automatically prevented so many important aspects of human life, not least the spiritual, from being studied. Central to enlightenment thought was the use and celebration of reason and the rational approach.

Humanity began to break out of the straightjacket of fixed and narrow-minded belief which had dogged the Middle Ages. These changes were very necessary and important in mankind's development. But, as always in human activities, they tended to go too far. Like a pendulum, humanity tends to swing from one extreme to the other and, as developing science began to move towards materialism, so spirituality and spiritual beliefs tended to become sidelined.

During the 18th and 19th centuries science and philosophy steadily moved more and more towards a materialistic interpretation of the world, whilst traditional religion strove to retain its mediaeval belief system which was becoming steadily undermined by new discoveries. Things seemed to be going very much in favour of the attitude of mainstream science until the middle of the 19th century, when what one can call the 'Psychic Renaissance' began.

The psychic renaissance – and the response

The activities of the Fox sisters in America in 1848 are often quoted as the trigger which initiated the renewal of interest in all things psychic. From this time onwards, interest and involvement in psychic activities, and an associated belief in survival, spread rapidly throughout America and Europe – greatly to the dismay of those who held to the materialist/humanist/rationalist view of life.

Regrettably, right from the beginning of this new wave of psychic activity, the reaction of the 'scientific establishment' was anything but logical and rational. Conan Doyle[8] recounts the cases of two American investigators who, initially sceptical and setting out to expose the mediumistic activities of the Fox family, eventually became convinced of the reality of the phenomena. Both of them published their conclusions in books and suffered for their temerity.

Professor Robert Hare, a well known chemist, was badly 'mauled' by his colleagues in the American Scientific Association and eventually resigned his chair at Harvard University.

Judge Edmonds, head of the High Court of New York, was forced to step down from his position.

When considering the evidence for survival a healthy, open-mindedly sceptical attitude, is most important. This is the proper scientific approach where nothing is accepted as real until all the evidence for and against has been properly investigated and assessed. Unfortunately, the majority of scientists and intellectuals at this time rejected the concepts of psychic phenomena and survival out-of-hand. They did this often without even considering the evidence available. To them, being entirely steeped in the materialist paradigm, and being frightened of what seemed to be a renewal of primitive and superstitious beliefs, the very idea of the paranormal appeared to be ridiculous and not worth considering, let alone investigating[2]. This was of course a totally unscientific approach and one which still remains today – although things are rapidly changing and the materialists are now fighting a rearguard action.

Attitudes to the paranormal in the 1880s to 1960s

A description of some of the attitudes and reactions to the paranormal that developed during the first 80 years or so of this period is of significance. In 1882 the Society for Psychical Research (SPR) was formed in London and for some years they supported or undertook significant research into many aspects of the paranormal. However, the SPR quickly became controlled by individuals with very sceptical views about survival. This led to, firstly, a very negative attitude towards all and everything psychic; and, secondly to the determination to uncover how mediums fraudulently produced the phenomena that they were supposed to demonstrate.

These lines of enquiry replaced the most important aspect: to investigate whether the phenomena were real or not. The 'logic' underlying this approach was that, from a materialist point of view psychic phenomena couldn't exist, therefore they didn't exist. Accordingly, anyone who believed otherwise, or who purported to practise psychic activities was either deluded, a fraud or a liar and had to be exposed for the public good. The outcome of this was that much of the activity of the SPR was concentrated on a 'crusade' to expose as frauds any and all mediums who came to their notice. This led to a great deal of controversy within the SPR between the sceptics and those with more open and objective attitudes. As a result, some of the latter resigned their membership.

Examples of prejudiced attitudes...

At the end of the 19th century the SPR employed as an investigator a young Australian lawyer, Richard Hodgson MA LLD (1855-1905), who was thoroughly sceptical in attitude and determined to expose the leading psychics of the day. He eventually became professor of legal studies at Cambridge University and was one of the co-founders of the American Society for Psychical Research. Examples of his approach follow.

(i) Mme Helena P. Blavatsky

Dr Hodgson was determined to make a reputation for himself as an exposer of fake mediums, but he didn't seem to have the right qualifications and experience to do the job properly. His first, so-called successful, big case was to investigate Mme Blavatsky, the leader of the Theosophical movement and a well-known medium. Blavatsky had manifested many physical phenomena and had received positive reports from preliminary investigations. The Society then delegated Hodgson to investigate her fully. His report stated that all she did was fraudulent and described a system by which she artificially produced her phenomena. However, his evidence was very tenuous, relying as it did largely on the testimony of a couple who had acted as Helena Blavatsky's servants and who had earlier been dismissed for a variety of misdemeanours. Although this report was scientifically unacceptable, it was taken up and published by the Society and Mme Blavatsky's reputation was accordingly severely damaged by its imputations. More recently, Dr Vernon Harrison has re-examined the 1885 Hodgson Report and concluded that "[it] should be read with great caution, if not disregarded...it is badly flawed and untrustworthy."[9]

(ii) Eusapia Palladino

Hodgson then undertook to expose Eusapia Palladino, an Italian peasant woman who was able to produce, whilst under trance, a wide range of quite remarkable physical phenomena. Again, he produced a report which appeared to demonstrate that Palladino was fraudulent but which, in reality, only exposed his own inability to accept the possibility of her psychokinetic abilities. This report was widely accepted, but in doing so the critics had to ignore the extensive testing in earlier years by some of the best researchers in

Europe (eg Lodge and Richet), who had clearly shown that Eusapia Palladino could produce genuine psychic phenomena.

(iii) Leonora Piper

Hodgson, however, met his match when he tried to expose the American medium Leonora Piper (see pp 14, 17, 98). Mrs Piper was one of the truly great mental mediums of the turn of the 19th and 20th centuries. Working through her control, Dr Phinuit, Mrs Piper over many years produced remarkably accurate material for the benefit of hundreds, if not thousands, of sitters. Although Dr Phinuit was something of a doubtful character, when other controls replaced him the information they produced remained extremely accurate. Through to the end of a very long working life there had never been any significant evidence of fraud from Mrs Piper.

However, Hodgson was determined to demonstrate that she was fraudulent and went to Boston to undertake an extensive investigation on her. Seeking to demonstrate that she was obtaining information about her sitters via normal channels, among other things he engaged private detectives to follow her, to check on everyone she met, and to intercept her mail. He also introduced his agents as false sitters into her sessions to trip her up. He got nowhere at all. Then a most dramatic event occurred.

A very good friend of Hodgson, George Pellew, died suddenly and his spirit took over as Mrs. Piper's control. Hodgson was thus in an unique position to ask many questions of Pellew about their own relationships and all the questions were answered accurately. Subsequently, Hodgson introduced many sitters, 30 of whom had known Pellew personally. So much accurate and confirmed information came from these sittings that Hodgson was converted to the spirit origin of Mrs. Piper's material – and thus also to a belief in survival. He wrote a report to the SPR stating these conclusions and explaining why he felt that his earlier reports had been wrong.

The final twist to this story came not long afterwards when Hodgson died unexpectedly at the early age of 50. Following his death he appeared as a control for Mrs. Piper, providing much useful information about the afterlife.

(iv) Leslie Flint

Another good example of the sceptical response of mainstream psychical investigators is that of Leslie Flint[10], probably the best known and most widely tested direct-voice medium of recent times. In the direct-voice phenomenon, material does not come through the medium's own vocal cords but via an ectoplasmic voicebox which forms separately from the body of the medium.

Flint was extensively tested by parapsychologists who, unfortunately, were not prepared to test him objectively but seemed determined to expose him as a fake. During the tests, Flint was tied up with hands and feet bound to his chair and his mouth thoroughly taped up – or even filled with water to prevent any speech. However, numerous voices still came through clearly. Whatever they tried to do, the researchers were unable to suppress his gift. They were reduced to suggesting more and more unlikely ways in which he was cheating, all of which were shown to be untenable. For example:

1   It was suggested that the voices were not real, but produced by a combination of hypnotic power on his part coupled with mass auditory hallucinations on the part of the sitters. This was disproved when the voices were tape recorded.

2 Another theory was that Flint was a ventriloquist. This was disproved when a throat microphone was attached to his throat so that the slightest sound coming from his larynx would be recorded. Nothing was recorded.

3   It was suggested that Flint could talk through his stomach! Quite how this could happen was not explained.

4 It was also suggested that he might have a two-way voice channel to another room where accomplices mimicked the voices of the departed, or that he might conceal tape recorders which would play prepared messages from the dead. That such mechanisms to fake voices would come nowhere near explaining the intricacies of what happened in his séances – particularly the fact that long two-way conversations often took place between the sitters and their deceased relations – never seemed to occur to these researchers. They believed implicitly that psychic phenomena couldn't exist and thus sought any explanation, however unreal, which could support their prejudices.

Leslie Flint was later investigated by another researcher, Professor William Bennett of Colombia University, who came to the conclusion that his direct-voice output was real.

Scientific attitudes during the late 19th and early 20th centuries

(i) Carpenter

The extremely negative and unscientific attitude of many of the individuals who were involved in psychical research during the late 19th and early 20th centuries is well summed up by some comments by Brian Inglis in his book *Natural and Supernatural*[2]. He is referring here to an academic called Dr W. Benjamin Carpenter who used his position and influence as professor at the Royal Institution in London [this reference has been corrected as "W.P. Carpenter was said to be at the Royal Institute"] to act in a way which, with hindsight, seems almost unbelievable. Unfortunately, there are still people of this calibre with influence who, perhaps more subtly, are still working in this way at the beginning of the 21st century. Quoting from Inglis (p 311):

> "The most unpleasant feature of all was the willingness of the scientific Establishment to condone smear tactics against the psychical researchers; a campaign in which Carpenter took the lead. His academic standing meant that his frequent contributions to the lay press appeared to carry the Establishment's *nihil obstat;* and his glib, self-confident style made them appear well informed, though he was in reality a chronic distortionist, incapable of arguing the case on its merits without falling back on verbal sleight-of-hand.
>
> The technique he adopted was significant not just for its influence at the time, but because it was to breed a swarm of imitators. The arguments he put forward sounded reasonable and were backed by evidence. But the arguments were rationalisations, and the evidence selected and if necessary twisted to fit the needs of his case for the prosecution".

This is very strong criticism of what was happening at the time.

(ii) Professor Charles Richet

Another criticism of such attitudes, more telling perhaps because of its source, can be found in a letter written by Professor Charles Richet to Baron Albert von Schrenck Notzing, both of whom were deeply involved in psychical research in the early years of the 20th century. The letter was written in response to the widespread criticisms of the validity of the materialisation phenomena which they had both been involved in investigating. It is printed on the final page of Schrenck Notzing's book[11]:

> "Criticism there must be; it is a condition of science itself. The truth must appear in its full beauty, but it will not happen through the agency

of incompetent and ignorant persons, who have seen nothing, controlled nothing, examined nothing; who have not even carefully read the accounts of the sittings. But it must come through savants who have really worked, who have experimented without cessation, and who prefer truth to probability."

(iii) Professor James Hyslop

A contemporary of Professor Richet was Professor James Hyslop who, starting as a sceptic, undertook much research which gradually convinced him of the reality of psychic phenomena and survival. Like Richet he was dismissive of many of his critics, saying:

"I regard the existence of discarnate spirits as scientifically proved and I no longer refer to the sceptic as having any right to speak on the subject. Any man who does not accept the existence of discarnate spirits and the proof of it is either ignorant or a moral coward. I give him short shrift, and do not propose to argue with him on the supposition that he knows nothing about the subject."[12]

(iv) Professor Hornell Hart

An example of how critics of survival have ignored available information in order to bolster their arguments is quoted by Professor Hornell Hart in his book *The Enigma of Survival* (see p. 8). He quotes three leading anti-survivalists from the first half of the 20th century who stated that an important argument against human survival was that no significant information about life after death had been given by mediums. These critics were Professor J.H. Leuba in 1916 (Leuba, J.H. *The Belief in God and Immortality*), Professor E.R. Dodds in 1934 (Proc. Soc. Psychical Res, 42, 147-172) and Anthony Flew in 1953 (Flew, A. *A New Approach to Psychical Research*. C.A. Watts, London). However, Hart carefully checked the literature and found that, by 1959, there were at least 63 books dealing with psychic communications on the nature of life after death. Of these, 25 were published before Leuba wrote his denial of the evidence, and another 25 were produced between 1916 and 1935 when Dodds published his denial. Since then, of course, much more material has become available. Thus we have the puzzle of the anti-survivalists denying the availability of evidence which in reality was readily accessible - if they were prepared to look for it. Hart also stresses that much of this evidence is significant and supported by associated verified psychic phenomena, and thus not easily dismissed.

(v) Professor Gary Schwartz's research

Unfortunately these comments, which come from the early period of psychic research, are closely paralleled by similar conclusions from recent years. Thus, Professor Gary Schwartz states in his book *The Afterlife Experiments* that:

> "Probably our greatest surprise and deepest disappointment was the unexpected discovery that some of the people who are most convinced that this entire subject is based on fraud were willing to criticize our work without even looking at our data."

But what is very interesting is that Schwartz admits that at an early stage of his research he was himself affected by the problem of extreme scepticism:

> "My degree of doubt in the presence of all data was frankly irrational. I was experiencing skeptimania. I knew it, but I hadn't been able to do anything about it."

(vi) Dr Victor Zammit's findings

A final recent comment which is very telling, in that it demonstrates the attitude of many scientists and intellectuals to the whole concept of psychical research and survival, is quoted by Dr Victor Zammit in his 1999 website[13]. He reports that, following a meeting with humanists in Sydney, Australia where he presented the objective evidence for survival, a typical sceptic said to him:

> "I would not believe in the afterlife even if you could prove it to me, Victor!"

This unknown individual is typical of the ultra-sceptics.

Dogmatic commitment to a materialist philosophy

Some people have very deep-seated psychological blockages which prevent them from even considering the possibility of anything beyond the purely physical universe. They appear to be completely closed-minded and are prepared to go to exceptional lengths to obliterate any case which goes against their own deeply held belief system. For that is what it is, simply a belief system – not factual reality backed up by real evidence.

They are the equivalent of religious fundamentalists or fanatics and behave in a similar way. As Professor Charles Tart has stated, such an approach is not truly scientific, it is what is called *scientism.* Scientism is a perversion of genuine science, being a "…dogmatic commitment to a materialist philosophy that 'explains away' the spiritual rather than actually examining it carefully and trying to understand it. Since scientism never recognises itself as a belief system, but always thinks of itself as true science, confusion between the two is pernicious."[14]

The problem with so many of these attempts to expose mediums as frauds was that, even when the attempts were unsuccessful or were later proved to have been wrong in their conclusions, the scientific establishment and the press were only too eager to latch on to the occasional doubts or the erroneous conclusions that had been made, even when these were corrected.

They also sought to denigrate both the individuals concerned and all mediums generally, on the basis of such minimal and faulty criticism. Regrettably, the media and many of the public were prepared to go along with so many of these 'fake exposures' and accordingly to give the whole of psychic research a bad name.

Fortunately, not everybody was seduced by this wave of rejection, ridicule and dishonesty which overwhelmed the scientific and intellectual world of the second half of the 19th century and the beginning of the 20th. There were a few courageous individuals, who having examined the evidence directly for themselves felt they had to speak out about the reality of what they had found.

Some became involved in research and investigation, adding to the body of sound evidence accruing in favour of survival. Often they accepted the reality of survival only after much inner turmoil. The evidence was clearly there – but it went against all their previous scientific training and background. The following were among the most prominent of these intellectually courageous individuals:

Sir William Barrett was a physicist who undertook research on hypnosis, telepathy, dowsing and death-bed visions. It was from his suggestion that the SPR developed.

Sir William Crookes, another famous physicist, was probably the first to undertake significant psychical research in the 1870s and later. His work with D.D.Home (see pp 13, 98) and Florence Cook (see p 14) is among the classics of psychical research.

Sir Oliver Lodge, a third well-known physicist of his time, investigated telepathy, automatic writing, trance speech and, particularly, the famous mediums Leonora Piper (see pp 14, 17, 98, 105) and Eusapia Palladino (see pp 14, 20, 104), demonstrating that their abilities were genuine.

Alfred Russel Wallace, the co-discoverer with Charles Darwin of the theory of evolution by natural selection, was one of the earliest workers to investigate mediumship and was involved with Crookes in the testing of Daniel D.Home (see above).

Professor James H. Hyslop was the focal point for the foundation and development of the American Society for Psychical Research. He was a leading investigator of the remarkable medium, Mrs. Piper (see above), and became a prolific researcher and writer particularly supporting the concept of survival.

There were also:

Lord Rayleigh, professor of physics at Cambridge, and **Sir J.J. Thomson**, the discoverer of the electron, who became involved in investigating psychical phenomena.

On the Continent there were a number of outstanding scientists and others who were prepared to look objectively at the strange phenomena which were being produced by a several well-known mediums and other sources of psychic material. Among these were:

Professor Charles Richet, the French Nobel Prize winner for physiology.

Baron Albert von Schrenck Notzing, a German physician who did very important work on ectoplasmic materialisations.

Professor Cesare Lombroso of the University of Turin.

Dr Gustave Geley, of Paris, who also provided valuable evidence for the phenomenon of materialisation, and

Professor Camille Flammarion, a French astronomer.

Opposing views: Scientific Materialism and Spiritual Hypothesis

In considering attitudes as to whether survival is a reality or not we have to look at two opposing philosophical systems or world views. These are, firstly, the mainstream scientific view which can be called scientific materialism or humanism or rationalism; and, secondly, we have what one may call the Spiritual Hypothesis[15]. In considering these two approaches to life we must remember that they are both essentially *belief systems* which, however widely held they may seem to be, should only be examined in the light of any available evidence in favour of their reality.

(i) Scientific materialism

Scientific materialism has given rise to what is usually called the philosophy of humanism or rationalism. For many people it seems to be a very bleak, even negative, view of life. In summary it suggests that the physical universe is all there is and that there is no spiritual reality beyond the workings of the human mind. It also maintains that the universe arose apparently from nowhere (or nothing), purely by chance, and that we know little about how this may have happened.

It proposes that there is no inherent meaning, purpose or value in creation. Further, that the natural world is simply a purposeless mechanism through which, by gradually increasing complexity, resulting from purely random interactions, life has arisen and eventually consciousness and self-consciousness have developed.

This philosophy also insists that self-consciousness and all the complex activities of the human mind are simply the results of the electro-chemical interactions of the vast numbers of nerve cells in our brains. In other words, mind and mental activity, which seem to many of us to be the primary reality in our lives, are just secondary spin-offs from the complex chemical interactions within our nervous systems. This very bleak, even pointless, interpretation of creation and life can perhaps be best summed up by some words written by **Bertrand Russell**, one of the great philosophers, mathematicians and humanists of the 20th century. He said in an essay written in 1932[16]:

> "Brief and powerless is Man's life; on him and all his race the slow, sure doom falls pitiless and dark. Blind to good and evil, reckless of destruction, omnipotent matter rolls on its relentless way."

Similar comments written by Russell in 1963 are even more negative, ending with the words: "Only on the firm foundation of unyielding despair, can the soul's habitation be safely built." [17]

A more recent critic of all things religious and spiritual is the 'evangelically outspoken' Neo-Darwinian biologist **Professor Richard Dawkins**. Like Russell, he believes that there is no purpose in life or evolution and no final end other than the slow running down of the universe due to entropy. In his book *River Out of Eden* he states chillingly:

> "Nature is not cruel, only pitilessly indifferent. This is one of the hardest lessons for humans to learn. We cannot admit that things might be neither good nor evil, neither cruel nor kind, but simply callous – indifferent to all suffering, lacking all purpose."[18]

The evidence for materialism

What is the evidence on which the materialist philosophy is based? It is suggested here that most of the evidence in favour of materialism is essentially circumstantial, that there is very little experimental scientific evidence which *directly* negates the spiritual approach to life. This is for the simple reason that the scientific method cannot prove a negative. Thus it cannot prove that God doesn't exist, it can only bring forward evidence that suggests that the existence of God is more or less unlikely.

Right from the start, as we have seen, science ignored all sorts of spiritual and moral matters, and thus gradually dug itself further and further into a materialist hole. Eventually, it was forced to concentrate on the humanist and rationalist interpretation of life. It rejected any alternative interpretations, simply because it had no way of including such approaches within its, rather limited, paradigm.

In following this path, the materialistic approach was forced to ignore or reject a vast range of human experience from the fields of religion and spirituality, for which, paradoxically, there is a growing body of both direct and indirect evidence. Thus, it is suggested here that scientific materialism is a belief system, arising from a set of assumptions based upon a particular interpretation of a range of scientific data, whilst ignoring much other evidence.

The present state of the materialist/humanist approach can perhaps be best summed up in a quote from William Thorpe, a well-known Quaker biologist of the middle of the 20th century, who wrote in his 1968 Swarthmore Lecture[19]:

> "All this…shows to my mind that the pessimistic outlook and conclusions of the Humanists, based as they often are on an outdated mechanistic view of the nature of evolution…are indeed unjustified and unjustifiable."

In rejecting or ignoring all the evidence, both experimental and circumstantial, which supports the spiritual view of life, the materialists tend to show attitudes of both closed-mindedness and arrogance. Regrettably, these are often well developed in those opposing a belief in the survival of death.

(ii) The Spiritual Approach

It has to be admitted that many religious people, particularly religious fundamentalists, are no less closed-minded or arrogant than their scientific counterparts. Nevertheless, there are many, and one hopes that most Quakers fall into this category, who are seeking for truth in an open-minded manner. After all, Quakerism is an experimental or experiential approach to life and thus in many ways resembles the scientific method at its best.

This is why the Spiritual Hypothesis is discussed here – it is the way of seeking for spiritual truth through experience, building up a spiritual philosophy as one moves through life and being prepared to modify and develop one's philosophy as new and valuable material becomes available. As in a scientific hypothesis, such material is tested and then rejected or incorporated into one's spiritual philosophy as seems right at the time.

The evidence for the spiritual hypothesis

So what is the evidence that makes the spiritual hypothesis more valid than the materialist hypothesis? This is summarised in a few points:

1 There is an enormous amount of evidence, admittedly largely anecdotal or circumstantial, from throughout the whole of recorded human history that a belief in a primary spiritual reality, call it God or what you will, has been held by probably more than 95% of people[20]. This evidence comes from religious, spiritual, mystical, cultural, anthropological and archeological sources. Many religions have become rather distorted from their original teachings as they evolved. Nevertheless, a spiritual approach to life seems to have been, and remains so today, an essential part of human nature for the great majority of the world's population[21]. To write this off as a primitive hangover from humanity's past, as so many sceptical materialists tend to do, shows, as already mentioned, a degree of ignorance and arrogance on their part. It is certainly an unscientific approach.

2 There is a significant amount of evidence from the healing research which has been undertaken during the past three or four decades[22]. Much of this has been done under strict scientific controls and the results point strongly towards mechanisms for healing which lie well beyond the limits of the materialist paradigm. In other words it supports the spiritual hypothesis.

3 Similarly, as has already been described in this bibliography, there has been much psychical research over the last 120 years, particularly that associated with survival, which again demonstrates the validity of the spiritual approach to life.

4 Finally, science is at last beginning to close the gap between science and spirituality after 300 years of growing separation. This trend is being led particularly by quantum physics, where well attested phenomena such as that of 'non-locality' demonstrate the inter-relationship of all creation[23]. Similarly, science has begun to investigate consciousness – a subject which was considered completely outside its remit until quite recently.

Attitudes at large. Media influence. A conspiracy?

In spite of all this, the general attitude towards survival and all things paranormal remains very negative. This is essentially because the firm grip that the sceptics have on the media ensures that any interesting stories in this field are either ignored or ridiculed.

A good example of this approach is that of Glen Hoddle when he was England's football coach a few years ago. Having admitted that he used a healer to cure injuries in his players (and also because of some of his personal philosophy which went along with this practice) he was totally destroyed by the hysterical response in the British national media.

These attitudes of the ultra-sceptics in science and the highly sceptical media have meant that serious survival research has essentially died out in the last 50 years or so[24]. Gifted mediums just keep their heads down and get on with helping those in need. They refuse to be investigated by people who have no desire to seek the truth, but just to confirm their own inherent prejudices[25].

For a long while, a very determined individual called Michael Roll (see p 10) has spent much time and effort in trying to publicise the evidence supporting the reality of survival[26]. He is convinced that there is a conspiracy between the churches, mainstream science, the media and the Establishment generally, to suppress the evidence supporting survival. He has circulated letters and pamphlets to many people to try to get his message across; but so far, apparently to little avail.

Whether or not there is an actual conspiracy is a matter for debate. The end result is certainly the rejection or ignoring of any evidence for survival and the suppression of any reasoned discussion, in the media or elsewhere, of what might be considered valid evidence.

The Ether (Void) and Survival

One of the foundations of the belief in a spiritual world which has been around for many centuries is the concept of the Ether. The Ether is an intangible reality which penetrates all matter and fills the whole of space. It enables electromagnetic waves to be transmitted through space. The Ether is the place where energy or a force-field exists in large amounts, although our physical senses are completely unaware of it.

Higher vibratory levels?

Because of the presence of the Ether, or the Void as it was known to the ancients, it is possible to conceive that the spiritual worlds could exist at 'higher vibratory levels' whilst overlapping with the physical universe. There is thus a place for both the physical and the spiritual to exist side by side.

If such an energy-dense Ether exists, penetrating the whole of the universe and if, as we now know, energy and matter are interchangeable, then it becomes possible to imagine how higher energies in the Ether can be the basis of higher, spiritual worlds integrated with, but invisible to, our own physical world.

The famous physicist, Sir Oliver Lodge, spent much of his career trying to promote this concept of the Ether as the place where energy exists, is stored in large amounts, yet remains apparently completely separate from physical awareness (see p 16).

Ether concept discredited. 19th and 20th centuries

Unfortunately, some experiments which took place in 1887 started to undermine the idea of the Ether. Two scientists, **Michelson and Morley**, attempted to measure the speed at which the Earth moved through the Ether of space. However hard they tried they were only able to obtain a zero result and, from this, they concluded that the Ether didn't exist. Subsequently, at the beginning of the 20th century, **Albert Einstein** constructed his theory of General Relativity which was based on assumptions that the Ether did not exist. Since then Einstein's theories have become the bedrock of modern physics and thus the concept of the Ether has been seemingly totally discredited, and has remained so for much of the last century. This enabled materialist scientists to state that any idea of a spiritual world had been totally undermined.

Ether and modern thought

However, things have been changing rapidly in recent years. In 1986 and 1992 independent experiments using modern techniques apparently showed that the Michelson-Morley experiments were flawed[27]. It was demonstrated that the Earth did move through the Ether of space and that it did so at an average speed of 350 kilometres per second.

Through this, the concept of the Ether has begun to be experimentally rehabilitated, although most mainstream physicists would not accept these conclusions. But there is more to this.

In recent decades, physics has demonstrated two important things:

Firstly, that gravitational measurements show that the amount of matter in the universe is not nearly enough to account for the way the universe is behaving. It has been calculated that around 95% of the matter in the universe is unobserved and may be unobservable. It has been called Dark Matter or Dark Energy because of this apparent invisibility.

Secondly, that space is not empty but is filled with what has been termed the Quantum Vacuum or the Zero-point Energy Field. Thus, as **Dr Edgar Mitchell**, the famous astronaut, has said in a recent lecture (May 2000), the Ether which was abandoned many years ago has been reincarnated by modern physics as the Zero-point Energy Field[28].

Anomalies in scientific theory. The "i-ther"

Over the past 15 years or so **Ronald Pearson**, a retired scientist and university lecturer (see p 10), has been working on a physical theory which overcomes the anomalies and problems which beset modern physics and cosmology. For example, there are significant anomalies in the Big Bang theory of the origin and evolution of the universe, and the fact that there are long-unresolved contradictions between the theory of relativity and quantum physics.

Pearson's researches, which appear to overcome these various anomalies, postulate an energy-rich background medium (or Ether) that he calls the "i-ther". The presence of this substrate, if validated, would provide a theoretical scientific underpinning for the vast amount of evidence for survival.

Unfortunately, Pearson's interesting and potentially very important work has been largely ignored or rejected by mainstream physics, probably because it calls into question a great deal of modern research and theory[29]

The gulf between science and spiritual belief is lessening?

Thus, what we appear to have in the universe is a small proportion of the total available energy existing as matter which we can see and measure. The remainder, and by far the largest proportion, exists as what are *at present* incomprehensible and un-measurable types of energy possibly existing on planes of being which are again beyond our understanding.

We can say that what is emerging from the developments of modern physics is a picture which is slowly becoming compatible with the ancient beliefs in a physical world interacting with a spiritual world. The physical world being a much smaller and ultimately less significant reality than the spiritual world.

We are beginning to find that the concepts of science and spiritual belief are slowly coming together.

The author's understanding of the relationship between matter and the spiritual world may be summarised as follows:

> Matter and the material world as we know them are essentially illusory, as has been taught by spiritual teachers over millennia.
>
> Matter, which gives the impression of solidity, is basically space and energy.
>
> All matter is composed of atoms which are again made up of subatomic particles.

Although called particles, the numerous subatomic structures within a single atom are minute packets of energy which are interacting with each other across what are the relatively large areas of space inside the atom. According to quantum physics, these minute packets of energy may behave either as particles or as waves. Individual atoms again interact similarly with others within molecules, and vast numbers of the latter go to make up the visible structures which we see as our world.

Thus the physical world is essentially a dance of myriads of minute packets of energy within what appears to be empty space, but which is actually an energy filled Ether: the Quantum Vacuum. It is out of this Vacuum that relatively small amounts of energy condense into what we, in our ignorance, call solid matter and, in our blindness, consider to be the only reality there is.

However, the true reality is far greater than this and exists both within and beyond the Quantum Vacuum. It includes those spiritual realms to which we all will pass when the time comes for us to shed our material bodies and move on to higher things.

Personal Conclusions

I have entitled this final section 'personal conclusions' since, because of the nature of the subject of survival and the evidence supporting it, people are likely to come to any one of a range of different conclusions depending on their backgrounds.

My background and particular interests

Every individual approaching the subject of survival comes to it with their own preconceived ideas about life and death and, as has been suggested above, these tend to influence how they interpret the evidence. What follows are my own personal conclusions derived from the evidence outlined in this bibliography and based on my background as a scientist and as someone who has been deeply interested and involved in spiritual matters for almost all my life. I have tried to be objective in my assessment, as far as that is humanly possible, bearing in mind that both spiritual wisdom and quantum physics suggest that all things are interconnected and thus real objectivity is not attainable.

The inextricably linked spiritual hypothesis and survival of death

I am led to the conclusion that the weight of evidence in favour of the spiritual hypothesis in general and of the survival of death in particular, *the two being inextricably linked,* is so great that it is only by ignoring, or denigrating large parts of this material, that the concept of survival can be rejected.

History shows that humanity is essentially a 'spiritually oriented' species. We have almost always understood that there is some greater reality than just ourselves and the material world, and have constantly sought after this reality in however illogical a manner. The following quotation seems to me to sum up the human situation:

> "We are not human beings following a spiritual path but spiritual beings following a human path."[30]

The recent Western belief, that there is nothing other than the material world, seems to me to be a minority and relatively transient view taking into account the whole of human experience in the past, present and, from the way things appear to be developing, seemingly into the future also.

Evidence in support of survival

The mass of evidence supporting survival is composed of accounts of many different events and investigations. Taken separately, almost all of these can be individually criticised by the sceptically minded in one or more ways.

The intention of the critics is to show that there are flaws in the observation or interpretation of the event, so that any conclusion supporting survival or other paranormal explanation must then be ruled out. However, when taken together as a whole, for me, the evidence forms an integrated, coherent and very considerable foundation, underpinning the concept of survival. It also provides a justification for the belief in survival which the great majority of humanity has held for millennia. Nevertheless, however strong the evidence for survival appears to be, it must be accepted that there is as yet, no absolute, incontrovertible evidence which provides an overwhelming case in its favour.

As I have stated above, whether we favour either the spiritual or the materialist hypothesis, for most of us, both must remain essentially belief systems until incontestable evidence becomes available. This, for the individual, may then convert one or other of these hypotheses into reality. Human experience suggests that *either:*

> awareness of this reality is only generated by rare events such as mystical experience, NDEs; *or*

> in the case of rare individuals like Swedenborg, Blake and Steiner, it is inborn.

Science, unfortunately, is unable to provide us with the ultimate answer to the question of survival. As I have tried to indicate earlier, science, although a wonderful way of seeking for truth, is unable to provide us with the certainties – the Truth – which most of us seek when following a spiritual path.

The final, personal, choice

The history of science provides many examples of theories apparently explaining how the world works which have had, ultimately, to be discarded or severely modified, as a result of subsequent discoveries. The final decision as to whether or not we accept the reality of survival must be an inner, individual choice. It will be based on personal experience, but supported by the work and experiences of others. Thus, we are given the choice between:

> the outwardly bleak, meaningless and mechanistic outlook of the materialist, humanist interpretation of life, – with, for me, its lack of any clear justification for this approach, *or*

the positive, meaningful and life-affirming philosophy of the spiritual hypothesis.

I find myself very much supporting the latter. Particularly as it is reinforced by a large body of direct and frequently explicit evidence[31].

At least the life-affirming hypothesis gives me a spiritual philosophy by which to live. It provides a meaning to life. It also leads to an explanation for, and understanding of, many of the events in life which otherwise may seem pointless and incomprehensible[32].

The information which has come from the research into survival provides humanity with the means and the justification to plot a more constructive and positive way ahead, rather than the blind and destructive path that we have been following for the past two or three hundred years. So, when seeking to come to a decision, we need to consider what I have termed "The Most Important Question" [33].

The Most Important Question

The most important question in life, because so much hangs on the answer, is this:

> *Which view of the universe, the spiritual approach or the material approach, best describes reality* and *which is redundant?*

I suggest that the evidence for survival, which is partly outlined in this bibliography, provides a sound basis for an answer in favour of the spiritual approach to life.

On a more light-hearted note, perhaps I may suggest the example of Pascal as one worth following in this context. **Blaise Pascal** was a seventeenth century French mathematician, theologian and man of letters who suggested that people should gamble on the possibility of God on the grounds that if they won, *they would win all,* while if they lost *there was nothing to lose!*

Similarly, acceptance of the concept of survival, with all that goes with it, provides us with a positive, purposeful context within which to live our lives. If we turn out to be wrong we will have lived happier, more meaningful lives but will go quietly into oblivion. On the other hand, if we are right, the whole of eternity is open to us and we will have placed our feet firmly on the path of return to the Source from which all and everything comes.

When the body dies…
The astral soul comes from the astral plane and returns to it.
The body comes from Nature and returns to it.
Thus everything returns to its own *prima materia*.

Paracelsus. *De Morbis Invis.*, iv

ॐ

The change from being to becoming seems to be birth,
and the change from becoming to being seems to be death,
but in reality no one is ever born,
nor does one ever die.

Apollonius of Tyana. *To Valerius*

ॐ

Birth is not a beginning;
Death is not an end.

Kwang Tse, xxiii, 9

Notes and References for Discussion and Conclusions

1 The material described in this bibliography is only a proportion of the books and reports published on the subject of survival. There is a great deal more, particularly in the psychical research journals. As Colin Wilson states in his book *Afterlife*: "...anyone who is willing to spend a few hours browsing through volumes of the Proceedings of the SPR (or its American counterpart) is bound to end with a feeling that further scepticism is a waste of time. Even if half the cases proved to be fraudulent or misreported, the other half would still be overwhelming by reason of sheer volume."

2 The development of psychic activities in the 19th and 20th centuries up to 1939 and the reactions of scientists and intellectuals to these phenomena are objectively considered in:

> Inglis, Brian (1977) *Natural and Supernatural. A history of the paranormal from earliest times to 1914* Hodder & Stoughton London and:

> Inglis, Brian (1984) *Science and Parascience. A history of the paranormal, 1914-1939* Hodder & Stoughton London

3 Quoted by Osis & Haraldsson (1997) (see p 86). Other authors have also spoken out against this explanation as an alternative to survival.

4 This discussion between Professor Braude, Montague Keen and Professor Peter Wadhams can be found on the International Survivalist Society website: www.survivalafterdeath.org

5 Professor Braude has considered the subject of survival and Super-psi in a number of recent publications. Some of his publications are:

> Braude, S. E. (1992) *Survival or Super-psi?* Journal of Scientific Exploration, vol 6(2)

> Braude, S. E. (2001) *Out-of-Body Experiences and Survival After Death* Int. J. Parapsychology, vol 12(1), pp 83-129

> Braude, S. E. (2003) *Immortal Remains: The Evidence for Life After Death* Rowman & Littlefield Lanham MD ISBN 0-7425-1471-4

This book, his most recent publication, brings together in detail all his earlier work and has been described by a reviewer as "Perhaps the best ever written assessment of the evidence for human survival of bodily death".

6 Wilson, Colin (1985) *Afterlife. An investigation of the evidence for life after death* Harrap London p 96

7 I have considered the topic of scepticism towards the evidence for survival at some length here and I make no apology for doing so. The ultra-sceptical attitudes widely demonstrated by those who should show a more open-minded sceptical approach have consistently been a block to any reasoned public debate on the subject over the past 140 years and thus need to be made more widely known.

8 Conan Doyle, Arthur (1930) *The Edge of the Unknown* John Murray London pp 274-279

9 Refer to HP Blavatsky and The Society for Psychical Research on www.theosophical.org.uk/27hpbspr.html

10 See:

Flint, Leslie (1971) *Voices in the Dark. My life as a medium* Macmillan London

11 Schrenck Notzing, Albert von (1920) *Phenomena of Materialisation* (see p 20).

12 Hyslop, James H. Quoted by Wilson, Colin (1985) see note 6

13 Dr Victor Zammit's website is:

http://www.ozemail.com.au/~vwzammit A Lawyer Presents the Case for the Afterlife.

14 Tart, C. T. (1999) *Science, scientism and the near-death experience* The Christian Parapsychologist, vol 13, no 7, pp 204-207

15 The concept of the Spiritual Hypothesis is not a new one having been put forward by other, earlier authors. I have considered this idea in:

Hodges, David (1994 and 2003) *Science, Spirituality and Healing* Friends Fellowship of Healing ISBN 1-873048-08-4

16 Quoted by Thorpe in note 19

17 It seems a strange contradiction that such a confirmed materialist as Russell can use the term 'soul' which, to most people, is a spiritually oriented term.

18 Dawkins, Richard (1995) *River Out of Eden* Weidenfeld & Nicolson London

19 Thorpe, William H. (1968) *Quakers and Humanists* Swarthmore Lecture (1968) Friends Home Service Committee London

20 This point is well illustrated by a paragraph from an article *"What is the True Reality?"* that I wrote for Quaker Forum (1999) part 1, pp 12 - 13 Thus:

> "The biologist Rupert Sheldrake has reminded us that throughout recorded history probably in excess of 95% of humanity has believed in some form of spiritual world-view and that it is only in recent times that this position has changed significantly. There are also many records from most cultures concerning individuals, usually saints and mystics but often ordinary people, who have had direct experience of spiritual reality. Christianity has a vast spiritual literature and this is repeated in all the great world religions. In the face of all this human experience, do we consider the spiritual approach to be just a mental aberration and turn instead to the modern interpretation of life found in scientific materialism – essentially the humanist approach; or do we accept the overwhelming weight of human experience and reject what is only a very recent interpretation of the human condition?".

21 Two recent examples of a continuing belief in God in the West are:

> In an article in a recent issue of the scientific journal *Nature*, almost 40% of American scientists have been reported to have a belief in God; and,

> between two-thirds and three-quarters of the British population maintain some sort of belief in the transcendent and the majority of these believe in a personal God. P. Brierley, ed. (1997) *UK Christian Handbook. Religious Trends* Christian Research Eltham London SE9. Similar results have been found from many opinion polls, particularly in America, over recent decades.

22 See, for example

> Benor, Daniel J. (1993) *Healing Research: Holistic energy medicine and spirituality* vol 1, Research in healing. Helix Editions Deddington Oxon UK. Republished (2001) in a new edition as:
> *Spiritual Healing. Scientific validation of a healing revolution* Healing Research, vol 1, Vision Publications Southfield MI USA ISBN 1-886785-11-2

Dossey, Larry (1993) *Healing Words. The power of prayer and the practice of medicine* Harper San Francisco CA USA

Hodges, R.D. & Scofield, A.M. (1995) *Is Spiritual Healing a Valid and Effective Therapy?* Journal of the Royal Society of Medicine vol 88, pp 203-207

23 The following books are just a sample of what has been published recently in this subject area:

Goswami, Amit (1993) *The Self-Aware Universe* Simon & Schuster London

Laszlo, Ervin (1993) *The Creative Cosmos* Floris Books Edinburgh

Clarke, C.J.S. (1996) *Reality Through the Looking-Glass* Floris Books Edinburgh Scotland

Radin, Dean (1997) *The Conscious Universe* HarperCollins San Francisco CA USA

Dossey, Larry (1999) *Reinventing Medicine* Element Books Shaftesbury Dorset UK

Schwartz, Gary & Russek, Linda (1999) *The Living Energy Universe* Hampton Roads Publ. Charlottesville VA USA

24 This comment really applies to research undertaken by the mainstream psychical research organisations; it does not apply to research in EVP and ITC (pp 25-27) which are flourishing across the world.

25 Mediums tend to refuse to be investigated not only because it is a waste of time, with the outcome usually being a denigration of their abilities. They also do it for their own personal safety, as two gifted materialisation mediums, Helen Duncan and Alec Harris, have died as a result of unexpected interruptions during a séance.

26 Michael Roll can be contacted at:

28 Westerleigh Road Downend Bristol BS16 6AH UK His website, the Campaign for Philosophical Freedom, is www.cfpf.org.uk

27 These results are quoted by R. D. Pearson in his book: *Intelligence Behind the Universe* The Headquarters Publishing Co., London (1990) ISBN 0-947823-21-2 Copies are available from Michael Roll at the above address. Ron Pearson's very interesting theories provide the basis for a modern concept of the Ether and its integration with quantum theory and are well worth reading, see note 29

28 The concept of the Quantum Vacuum/Zero-point Energy Field is well discussed from a spiritual point of view by:

> Davidson, John (1989) *The Secret of the Creative Vacuum. Man and the energy dance* C.W. Daniel Saffron Walden Essex UK ISBN 0-85207-202-3

Another, more recent, book which considers the Quantum Vacuum/ Zero-point Energy Field in some detail – but very readably – is:

> McTaggart, Lynn (2001) *The Field. The quest for the secret force of the universe* HarperCollins London ISBN 0-7225-3764-6

29 As well as Ronald Pearson's book *Intelligence Behind the Universe*, note 27, his other publications are available from Michael Roll at the address in note 26. The list of publications and much further information can be found on the website of the Campaign for Philosophical Freedom:

> www.cfpf.org.uk

30 This quotation has been attributed to the Quaker John Wilhelm Rowntree (1868-1905) but I have been unable to confirm this.

31 Scientific materialism does not, and is seemingly unlikely to be able to, provide us with and answers about where the universe came from, or how it originated and where it will end up. On the other hand, the spiritual hypothesis plus survival research, as indicated here, provides at least in outline, a coherent picture of who we are, where we come from and where we are going.

32 Not only does the material described here give meaning and purpose to this life, it also provides us with a reasonable and coherent description of what happens after death and subsequently. Although many of the reports describing life after death may vary considerably in detail, overall, they provide a very similar picture of what the 'spiritual realms' are like, enabling anyone willing to study the subject to come to reasonable conclusions about life after death.

33 Hodges, David (2002) *The Most Important Question* The Friend (19 July 2002 p 19)

Short Reading List

Although covering only a proportion of the available literature on the survival of death, the list given above remains rather extensive and contains much material which may seem rather daunting to those without the time or expertise to tackle it. Accordingly the following short reading list is suggested to provide an overview of the subject by selecting a few of the more readable and straightforward books from each of the main sections of the bibliography. The material included here must be considered only as an introduction to the subject, not as a detailed coverage. For details of publishers, etc., please refer to the references in the main body of the text.

1 Introductory References

> Ellison, Arthur (1988) *The Reality of the Paranormal* Guild Publishing
>
> Brookesmith, Peter (1989) *Survival of Death* Macdonald
>
> Johnson, R.C. (1953) *The Imprisoned Splendour* Hodder & Stoughton. And (1984) *Light of All Life* Pilgrim Books
>
> Wilson, C. (1985) *Afterlife* Harrap

2 Direct Research

> Inglis, Brian (1977) *Natural and Supernatural* Hodder & Stoughton
>
> Inglis, Brian (1984) *Science and Parascience* Hodder & Stoughton
>
> These books provide summaries of most of the research undertaken over almost 100 years
>
> Solomon, Grant & Jane (1999) *The Scole Experiment* Judy Piatkus

3 Indirect Research

> (a) Reincarnation research
>
> Cranston, Sylvia (1998) *Reincarnation* Theosophical University Press
>
> Hall, Judy (2001) *Way of Reincarnation* Thorsons
>
> Stevenson, Ian (1987) *Children who Remember Previous Lives* University of Virginia Press
>
> Stevenson, Ian (1997) *Where Reincarnation and Biology Intersect* Praeger

(b) Research into Out-of-the-Body and Near-Death Experiences

    (i) OBEs

        Muldoon, Sylvan J. & Carrington, Hereward (1992) *The Projection of the Astral Body* Rider.

        Monroe, Robert (1972) *Journeys Out of the Body* Souvenir Press

    (ii) NDEs

        Morse, Melvin & Perry, Paul (1992) *Transformed by the Light* Villard Books

        Eadie, Betty (1995) *Embraced by the Light* Thorsons

        Bailey, Lee W. & Yates, Jenny (1996) *The Near-Death Experience. A Reader* Routledge

(c) Research into Past-Life Regression

    Wambach, Helen (1979) *Reliving Past Lives* Hutchinson

    TenDam, Hans (2003) *Exploring Reincarnation* Rider

    Newton, Michael (1996) *Journey of Souls* Llewellyn Publications

    Bowman, Carol (1997) *Children's Past Lives* Element Books

4 Seers and Mystics

    Stanley, Michael (1988) *Emanuel Swedenborg* Crucible

    Fox, Leonard & Rose, Donald (1996) *Conversations with Angels* Chrysalis Books

    Raine, Kathleen (1965) *William Blake* Longmans, Green

    Wilkinson, Roy (1993/94) *Rudolf Steiner Aspects of his spiritual world view* (three short volumes) Temple Lodge Publishing

    Bro, Harmon (1989) *Edgar Cayce* Aquarian Press

5 Shamans and Shamanism

    Drury, Neville (1989) *Elements of Shamanism* Element Books.

    Rutherford, Leo (1996) *Thorsons Principles of Shamanism* Thorsons

6 The Experiences of Mediums

    Cummins, Geraldine (1932) *The Road to Immortality* Nicholson & Watson

Sherwood, Jane (1964) *Post-Mortem Journal* Neville Spearman and (1992) *Peter's Gate* C.W. Daniel

Greaves, Helen (1969) *Testimony of Light* World Fellowship Press and (1974) *The Wheel of Eternity* C. W. Daniel

Praagh, James Van (1999) *Reaching to Heaven* Judy Piatkus

7 The Study of Death and Dying

Kübler-Ross, Elisabeth (1991) *On Life After Death* Celestial Arts and (1997) *The Wheel of Life* Bantam

Osis, Karlis & Haraldsson, Erlendur (1997) *At the Hour of Death* 3rd edn Hastings House

Miller, Sukie (1998) *After Death* Touchstone

Index

135